CRITIQUE OF PURE EDUCATION

A PHILOSOPHY FOR THE CHRISTIAN HOME EDUCATOR

CRITIQUE OF PURE EDUCATION

A PHILOSOPHY FOR THE CHRISTIAN HOME EDUCATOR

ROBERT W. WATSON

Tampa, Florida

The views and opinions expressed in this book are solely those of the author and do not reflect the views or opinions of Gatekeeper Press. Gatekeeper Press is not to be held responsible for and expressly disclaims responsibility of the content herein.

CRITIQUE OF PURE EDUCATION:
A Philosophy for the Christian Home Educator

Published by Gatekeeper Press
7853 Gunn Hwy., Suite 209
Tampa, FL 33626
www.GatekeeperPress.com

Copyright © 2023 by Robert W. Watson

All rights reserved. Neither this book, nor any parts within it may be sold or reproduced in any form or by any electronic or mechanical means, including information storage and retrieval systems, without permission in writing from the author. The only exception is by a reviewer, who may quote short excerpts in a review.

Library of Congress Control Number: 2023938450

ISBN (paperback): 9781662939389
eISBN: 9781662939396

All quotations from the Scriptures are from the text of the Holy Bible, commonly known as the Authorized King James Version.

In chapter 8, for quotations from the NIV:
Scripture quotations marked (NIV) are taken from the Holy Bible, New International Version®, NIV®. Copyright © 1973, 1978, 1984, 2011 by Biblica, Inc.™ Used by permission of Zondervan. All rights reserved worldwide. www.zondervan.com The "NIV" and "New International Version" are trademarks registered in the United States Patent and Trademark Office by Biblica, Inc.™

"The Educator and Cultural Reclamation"
Copyright © 2002 by James E. Kibler.

"Watson's modest volume faces hard facts and gives proper warnings. His is a prophetic book that takes its authority from a broad vision of wholeness and the elegant simplicity of good common sense. It is one of those books that has the potential to do immense good."
....
—DR. JAMES E. KIBLER, Author of *Our Fathers' Fields: A Southern Story*

CONTENTS

Preface	1
Apologia	5
1. Goals: Substance and Evidence of Pure Education	17
2. Foundations: American Schools and Industrialism	29
3. Foundations: The Home School and Independence	45
4. Foundations: The Home School and Culture	59
5. Manners: The Fine Art of Living	71
6. Work and Leisure: The Forgotten Arts	87
7. The Curriculum: The Means of Pure Education	103
8. The Curriculum: Enriching the Heart with the Bible	115
9. The Curriculum: Enriching the Soul with Literature	129
10. The Curriculum: Enriching the Soul with Art and Music	143
11. The Curriculum: Enriching the Mind with Rhetoric	153
12. The Curriculum: Enriching the Mind with Moral Philosophy	167
13. The Curriculum: Enriching the Mind with Mathematics	179
14. The Curriculum: Enriching the Senses with the Sciences	191
Final Thoughts	205
Appendix: The Educator and Cultural Reclamation	209

PREFACE
To the Third Edition

When the first and second editions of *Critique of Pure Education* were published in 2000 and 2002, respectively, I offered my belief that the home is the only legitimate institution to educate anyone. After twenty years, this statement remains just as valid today as it was then—in fact, more so. While local churches may arguably have a teaching ministry, it is certain that civil governments have absolutely no legitimate claim to educate a single child.

With this third edition, I am more convinced than ever that public education is a continuing, malicious fraud that must be eliminated if Americans ever hope to enjoy liberty again. Frankly, I wonder about the fitness of parents who willingly subject their precious children to critical race theory, gender confusion, pornography, and a host of other evils prevalent in the schools that have no relationship to education whatsoever. Indeed, a case can be made that the current agenda in tax-supported schools is simply child abuse. Those who continue to perpetrate the fraud of public education ought to be marked as contemptible, whether the fraudster is a politician, a teacher, or a parent.

We have heard so often, thanks to bureaucrats and journalists, how the ills of society can be cured with "more education." According to the pundits, with just a little more education, our social problems will be wondrously eradicated. As a supposed universal panacea, "more education" has become fixed in the American psyche and is a maxim of unquestionable validity. In fact, as a tenet of faith, the doctrine of more education has allowed charlatans to deceive the simple, to plunder the common treasury, and to coerce the unenlightened. Implicit with more education is the notion of reforming habits. If the civil government can reform its citizens by instilling "good" habits through sufficient education—as Plato suggests—then the just State will emerge. However, call it whatever you wish, this reforming of citizens, particularly youngsters, for purposes of the State fails to be *education*.

Herein lies the deceitfulness of "correcting" the governmental system. One cannot correct or reform an illegitimate activity that falls outside the proper role of civil government. By usurping a rightful function of the home, the governmental minions (politicians, school boards, teacher unions, PTOs, and textbook publishers) will fail with any so-called reform and will only increase the frustration of teachers and students alike. However, educational success is never the goal of centralized governments. One would think this to be the case when school administrators piously talk about educating children. While I will be the first to admit that many young people become teachers because they genuinely wish to make a difference in the lives of children, most of the really talented folks leave the public sector very quickly, recognizing that their talents are wasted. What the governmental system has become is a haven for not-so-brilliant professionals who are afraid of the union's mafia and who are holding out long enough to retire on a state pension. This is hardly the stuff that one would consider to be dedication or even a calling.

The question naturally arises: "If the governmental system cannot be reformed, what can I do about the mess?" The biblical principle is to separate from evil and to abandon it. In reality, the question that parents should be asking themselves is this: "What are we expecting as a result of education?" The answer should be simple. The final educational product ought to be either a lady or a gentleman, who leads by example and who becomes part of the leisure class. This is what Thomas Jefferson envisioned, and the antebellum South tried to implement Jefferson's ideas. In a real sense, home education is the revival of this humane Southern education, with its emphasis on the liberal arts and moral philosophy, and home scholars are becoming the new modern gentry. These young people have the benefit of avoiding a governmental miseducation, and therefore they have the rare ability to think critically. Home educators have proven that when education is the goal, not vocational or social training, students can excel on low budgets without the help of so-called experts. Of course, any talk about a gentry will raise a hue and cry of inequality and a false concern for the poor.

Let me make it perfectly clear: the central, state, and local politicians, along with the educational (falsely so-called) bureaucracy, could not care less about any child's education, whether the youngster is rich or poor. Children do not vote, and they can safely be ignored politically. The various teacher unions have failed both teachers and students, because the unions are politically motivated to undermine the entire system through Marxism. The governmental common school lives, moves, and has its being by acquiring more power to control—and not to educate. And yet Americans are always wondering why their money-devouring school systems are producing such shallow, mediocre examples of humanity. The best the bureaucrats can provide to a bewildered herd of taxpayers is a scheme of standardized testing and more teacher accountability. In other words, more failure leads to more control.

This book is dedicated to the proposition that all human beings (which includes children) instinctively desire to be free. I have difficulty in taking seriously the sanity of modern Americans who say they are a free people and declare it with straight faces. How in the name of common sense can Americans possibly claim to be free when they fail to enjoy the full benefits of their own labor, when the central government takes 25 to 30 percent directly from their paychecks, when the bank owns their houses, their lands, and their cars, when the public school claims to own their children, when materialism owns their souls, and when they are afraid to disagree morally with their bosses in order to keep their dehumanizing jobs? The first step toward regaining the freedom that has been lost over the past several years is by offering to your children the liberty to learn in the environment of the home where they belong, and not in the confines of an indoctrination cell called a public classroom.

There are a few minor changes to the text in this edition from the previous ones. Some terminology has been updated, and a few thoughts have been expanded. However, the principal arguments remain the same. because they are based on time-honored concepts. Also, Dr. James E. Kibler's fine essay, "The Educator and Cultural Reclamation," which appeared in the second edition as the introduction, is the appendix to this volume.

ROBERT W. WATSON

APOLOGIA

Friends, Romans, countrymen, lend me your ears;
I have come to bury Caesar, not to praise him.

—WILLIAM SHAKESPEARE, *The Tragedy of Julius Caesar*

Men, brethren, and fathers, hear ye my defence which I make now unto you.

—ACTS 22:1

I hope this book will ignite honest and thoughtful discussion about the philosophical moorings for home education. I can only hope and pray that the ideas espoused on these pages are thoughtfully weighed. Indeed, I would find great satisfaction in knowing that home educators have at least begun to think about establishing a set of objective values in their schools, which provide for security and stability of purpose. Home education is not a new phenomenon, because home schools have naturally existed since the days of Adam and Eve. If this is so, then why do we need a specific philosophy for the home school? I fear that most home educators are teaching by instinct, not by knowledge. While this instinct is right and proper, parents have some powerful foes, who will become increasingly less tolerant and will never be convinced by any argument, especially if the argument is based solely on parental instincts.

However, even though the oppressors may never concede mentally to the independent educator, parents should be able to provide rational reasons for the superiority of home education to the public. After all, the general public forms the strongest political lobby of all—*public opinion*. Politicians, particularly corrupt ones, quickly follow and drift along the current of public opinion, and if public opinion shifts in favor of home education, watch the politicians clamor to show their support for "all those bold and courageous families." I truly believe that home educators have the opportunity to create the next generation of leaders in government, education, and culture. However, this accomplishment will be done only if home educators can articulate their instincts into explicit values.

I have written this book because I believe home education represents the best expression of economic, political, social, and spiritual freedom. Since most Americans concern themselves only with the trivial details of living, those who begin to reflect deeply about life and its fundamental principles must be prepared to defend their position for not being superficial like the crowd. While everyone will occasionally think about a knotty issue such as truth, purpose, death, or eternity, the transient philosopher gives up shortly after beginning to think. If discovering anything during their ponderings, typical Americans realize very quickly that rational thinking is difficult. The true philosopher sticks with the problem and tries to reconcile any conflicting issues. The goal of the philosopher is to discover the essential principle that is the glue that keeps the physical, the intellectual, the spiritual, and the emotional worlds together. If the American home-school movement fails, the failure will rest upon our lacking a viable educational philosophy and upon our adopting incorrect assumptions about education.

The work of a philosopher is a thankless task, which Socrates discovered as he defended himself in an Athenian court many centuries ago. Since the days of Socrates, philosophers worth their weight in hemlock have caused folks to become uncomfortable. This uneasiness is the result of the philosophers asking probing questions about issues that were believed to have been settled—at least, settled from an individual's point of view. All of us resent the upsetting of our comfortable worldviews. Everyone holds certain assumptions about life, which cannot be proved or disproved. In other words, assumptions are our self-evident axioms that support our views about life and living. We adopt these assumptions from various sources—family, school, church, and government. Yet whenever anyone threatens these sincerely held beliefs, we tend to buckle up and stand our ground. This defense is good, because convictions ought to be defended. But often, the defense is not for our assumptions at all, but rather for accepted ideas that can be modified or even eliminated without upsetting our core beliefs. Having to rethink our accepted ideas about social institutions, patriotism, and life's goals, to name a few, creates mental turmoil until balance once again achieves equilibrium.

My assumptions in life are few. In fact, I have only three. First, I believe that God is alive and well. Second, God communicates with us in the same way that we communicate with other people, which is with *words*. And third, God has given to us His words, which are infallible and complete, written in a book that we can personally hold in our own hands, read with our own eyes, and study in our own language. Thus, this critique will reflect my belief that absolute truth exists in the world and that anyone can discover this truth easily. Other than the above three assumptions, I deal with facts. If anyone tells me that Russian roulette is a wholesome and harmless game, he had better have some strong evidence for why I should believe him. Also, I refuse to accept the assumption that a governmental teacher can do a better job with education than a mother can, unless the proponent is ready to offer tangible proof for this belief. Otherwise, I will place this person in the same category as the promoter of Russian roulette—a madman dangerous to decent society.

I must define two terms, which I have coined. First, by *pure education* I mean the transfer of valuable ideas to students, when these ideas lead students toward more wisdom, and when this wisdom helps students to enrich their culture. Thus, the student first imitates and then enriches. Even though it is reasonable to expect the student's imitation will be patterned only after the best ideas and arts, pure education does not merely preserve the student's culture. Enrichment implies betterment, which adds value to life for everyone. Pure education makes the world intelligible, which sustains students and which permits them to become active participants in the world, thus enriching others in their sphere of influence. On the other hand, technical training fails to be education, because the main concern of training is the transfer of processes, or rote answers, not ideas. Indeed, not only is technical knowledge void of ideas, but this training is incapable of preserving any culture as well.

Second, *culturalism* is a word that I use as opposed to industrialism. While I shall explain more about culturalism in chapter

4, I will merely say at this point that culturalism is the belief that human beings instinctively desire permanence and meaningful values during their lifetimes and for future generations.

Since pure education should enrich students with truth and knowledge in the context of their culture, I shall argue that education exists legitimately as a cultural and familial institution, not primarily as a religious one. This is not to say the Bible is not important. On the contrary, the Bible is necessary for pure education to take place. In addition to the above, I shall also argue that the conflict between the state boards of education and the home schools is not humanism against Christianity, but rather vocational training versus pure education. If this is true, then all governmental, most private, and many home schools are not educating anyone. While I reluctantly use the terms *public education* and *Christian education*, these two activities are in reality *not* education; better terms would be public and Christian *training*. However, while some schools may approximate education, the home school is the only institution capable of providing pure education. This is the purpose of this book: to provide a standard by which home educators can ensure that the activity in the home school is indeed education.

Even though my sympathies lie with Christian educators, I make no apology for my rough treatment of Christian schools. My harshness is because Christian educators and philosophers have been too sloppy with their vocations. In some small way, I hope that the reading of this book may help salvage some of the schools. However, I am not holding my breath. Whenever I mention Christian schools in this book, I am referring to the elementary, middle, and high schools, not to the colleges, which is a different subject, and which would require a separate book. For the most part, Christian schools are abject, dishonest failures, continuing to rob parents not only of their money but also of the souls of their children. Of course, even though one can question the improper motives of some pastors, who use church schools to build their ministries, no one denies that Christian educators intended to be a blessing and a help to families and never meant to harm anyone. But for over seventy years, the good intentions have now been weighed in the balances and have been found woefully wanting.

To be sure, the professors of education in the Christian colleges trained teachers and administrators, but the graduates were armed only with the secular pseudoscience of psychology and with superficial platitudes like "keep Christ in the subject matter" and "train soul-winners to go into the workplace." As part of their insubstantial efforts, the Christian educational philosophers stated that the Bible should be the foundation for Christian schools. If this were true, then how do we explain the collapse of Christian schools on such a firm foundation? In reality, with little critical thought, Christian leaders adopted the same foundation, the same ends, and the same forms, methods, and structure from the public schools. Even the major Christian educational publishers promulgated the public school mentality with their textbooks and objective tests. In short, today the vast majority of Christian schools, state-certified or not, are simply extensions of the public schools.

Some readers may think that the arguments in this book rely heavily upon the belles lettres, history, and economics, rather than upon philosophical reflection. Seeing that philosophers since the pre-Socratics have failed to offer one single answer about the business of life, I see no need to rely upon their endless speculations. Therefore, whenever I speak about philosophy, I do not refer to the discipline that tries to justify faith through human reason and logic, but rather I mean a system of values and beliefs that guides one's personal actions. My project as expressed in this critique attempts to provide such a system of values. Our values include those that are economic, social, political, epistemological, religious, and aesthetic. Of course, these values and beliefs come from many sources of knowledge, and not just from the human mind and logic, which are in the domain of philosophy.

Also, some readers will think that some ideas in this book are anti-capitalistic. There is a reason for this perception. I do not oppose capitalism per se; however, I do oppose a capitalism that is centralized and financial, which has nothing to do with efficiency. Without doubt, economic well-being is a highly prized value in the modern Western world. Since capitalism offers incentives for profit, the American economy has produced the highest standard of living in history ever. However, many citizens—some who should know better—confuse capitalism with owning productive property. Capitalism is not an end but a systematic process, a means. Like any other amoral process, capitalism derives its ethics from human beings. Since private enterprise is a natural human desire, this desire can become either good or evil, depending on the ethics of the person. Capitalism works well only when moral people use the process.

On the other hand, ownership of productive property is not a process but a natural right of every human being. Without the ability to own property, any discussion about freedom of speech, religion, or association becomes meaningless. Without productive land, the individual is deprived of the very means of life itself.

Not only have I tried to avoid the language of philosophers in this book, but I have limited the use of terms found in educational literature as well. However, I should at least reveal my educational values and beliefs to the reader. In educational jargon, teachers are divided into four tidy philosophical groups: essentialists, perennialists, progressivists, and reconstructionists. One can argue that these groups are a little too tidy. Indeed, in *Education in the Truth*, Norman De Jong asserts that the classifications are wrong, because he believes Christians are radical, conservative, and liberal all at once. While this may be true, De Jong's thought here fails to help when trying to formulate a viable philosophy of pure education. While I usually ignore labeling because the categories of ideas are often artificial, there is some merit to these philosophical classifications.

Without hesitation, I declare that I am an unabashed essentialist. This makes me, according to Theodore Brameld in his *Education as Power*, a reactionary and, no doubt, dangerous to the national educational system. Nevertheless, as an essentialist, I posit that teachers are responsible for transmitting truth that is essential for the next generation. This position means that I value two things above all else: first, the individual student, who is uniquely gifted; and second, my regional culture, which I received from the past. Thus, education is for self-enrichment of the student and not for the benefit of society in general. Insisting that education is for cultivation, and not for vocation, the essentialist educates the whole student, who benefits mostly through private tutoring.

The curriculum is primarily the reading of literature, history, and moral philosophy and the exercising of rhetoric through writing and oratory. The student is examined by oral examinations and by

Apologia

writing papers expressing argument, not by objective tests revealing a good memory. Also, as an essentialist, I have an end for my teaching, which is the cultivation of individual students who enjoy learning for the mere sake of learning and who are able to govern themselves well. Thus, pure education is demonstrated through the substance of learning ideas and by the evidence of purposeful living. In short, essentialism produces leaders.

On the other hand, both the perennialist and progressivist fail to have goals. The perennialist is satisfied with the status quo and wishes to conserve whatever culture is in vogue, which makes the next-generation perennialist a progressivist by default. If one wonders why so-called conservatives seem to become more liberal as time goes by, herein is the reason: the status quo is merely defended, and conservatives fail to have a plan for taking back lost ground. The perennialist respects tradition, so long as it is not too far in the distant past. The perennialist is unmistakably a progressivist, but only at a very slow rate of speed.

The progressivist believes in forward progress—the faster, the better—which has no end and maintains no culture. On the other hand, the reconstructionist desires to use the schools to remake society. The focus is upon the collective, which will be governed by the democratic majority. Since the individual is no longer unique, social and technical training, not education, takes place in classrooms with instruction given to groups of students according to their age. Therefore, reconstructionism produces followers. Nevertheless, reconstructionists do have a goal, which makes them and essentialists similar in this one respect. I shall discuss the goals of pure education further in chapter 1.

The structure of this book follows a logical sequence. First, I must establish the goal of pure education. This is the most important issue when trying to offer reasons for educating our children in the first place. *Why do we educate?* There must be a better answer than "because the government said so." Next, I shall discuss the first principles, or metaphysics, of education, which is called foundations. As I have already stated, I shall argue that the primary conflict in the American schools today is not religious but institutional. Then, before I delve into the means to the goal, I have devoted one chapter each to manners and leisure. Most educational philosophies ignore these vital elements of learning, which is not surprising, because manners and leisure no longer have an educational meaning to technological Americans. I shall argue that students of pure education are first and foremost ladies and gentlemen, and these cultured young people understand the difference between leisure, labor, and wasting time. Finally, I have written several chapters about the curriculum in general and the subject matter in particular for pure education. These chapters will discuss the importance of enriching students through their heart, soul, mind, and senses, or in other words, the importance of enriching the whole person.

If this book is a blessing to you, then the Lord Jesus Christ must receive all of the glory. My thoughts represent a synthesis of what I believe to be truth. Like all human beings, I am a product of the ideas that I have read and heard. While most of the ideas in this critique have been credited when credit could be given, the analysis and conclusions are my own. Thus, any defects in logic must be placed upon my shoulders, for I alone bear the blame. I am a poor

Apologia

instrument of God's grace with only ordinary gifts. I struggle with words like any writer, and my thoughts may be unclear at times. Nevertheless, the ideas in this book represent my expressed admiration for home education—the rebirth of a free America.

01 GOALS
Substance and Evidence of Pure Education

Fair is foul, and foul is fair:
Hover through the fog and filthy air.

—WILLIAM SHAKESPEARE, Macbeth

Beware lest any man spoil you through philosophy and vain deceit, after the tradition of men, after the rudiments of the world, and not after Christ.

—COLOSSIANS 2:8

Why do your children go to school? This question is both to you personally and to us collectively as Americans. Perhaps you believe Francis Bacon's dictum, *Ipsa scientia potestas est*, or in English, "Knowledge itself is power." This statement is paraphrased in quips like, "I want my children to have a better life than I had," or "I want my children to be able to get good jobs." For the most part, Americans have espoused Friedrich Nietzsche's idea of the superman, which posits that leadership naturally belongs to the powerful.

Therefore, most power seekers would reason that if knowledge is power, then the more education one has, the more powerful one will become. But as many PhDs have discovered, being "over-qualified" can be a curse when honest labor is denied them. Sometimes, simply wanting to make a little extra money, or trying to find any kind of work during hard times, leaves highly-educated men and women in desperate straits. Perceiving that their jobs, positions, or companies could be in danger of being taken over by the "superior, natural leaders," foremen and bosses tend to become paranoid and refuse to hire these "powerful" job seekers.

However, most schools, with their emphasis on technical training, fail to empower students, but rather enslave them, because the learning of processes cannot generate ideas. Without ideas, the student will readily accept the so-called superman's calling evil, good, and good, evil. This ethic of "fair is foul" is the prerogative of Nietzsche's supermen, who refuse to abide by the ethics of the weak, which of course to them is Christian morality. In fact, the weak ought to be eliminated. Undoubtedly, Nietzsche believed that his supermen possess a different kind of knowledge other than the technical kind, which merely gives human beings a minimal competency to count change or to push buttons on a machine. Nietzsche's power is not equated with knowledge but with ideas. Without ideas, American students walk blindly in thick fog and are powerless to fight any moral battle, much less to determine what is fair and foul.

Not surprisingly then, most educators, whether home, private, or governmental, fail to know why they take time to teach. While they may have some vague feelings about getting their students ready for college or preparing their students to compete in the

1. Goals: Substance and Evidence of Pure Education

world marketplace, these ideas stop short of being specific. Like a good thesis statement, which provides focus and clarity to an essay, a goal is absolutely necessary to ensure direction toward the intended end. Purposeless educators, like their students, are in a fog and will revolve in circles, turn upside down, and eventually crash, because they have become disoriented by the vertigo.

Even though typical governmental teachers are enveloped by this bewildering fog of vague outcomes, apologists for public schooling have plenty of books in print to keep no one ignorant of their stated goals. In *Education as Power*, Theodore Brameld, founder of social reconstructionism, offers plenty of insight. The goal of public education, according to Brameld, is to create a union of nations, that is, a one world order. Even though he died in 1987, Brameld is still held in great esteem among educationalists. In fact the former Boston University professor and a signer of the Humanist Manifesto had lectured in many foreign countries about education under the sponsorship of the U.S. State Department. While his ideas were roundly criticized at first, fifty years after *Education as Power* was published, social reconstructionism has become the norm in the public school systems. If the goal of the public school in America is to prepare the student to be a model citizen for world democracy, then the system is a resounding success, because most graduates are docile subjects of the civil government, ready to take their menial positions under the elite in the industrial-governmental cartel and willing to believe the mass media without any critical thought about the message. Reconstructionists know where they are heading, because they have the confident belief in world democracy. This confident belief is called faith.

Indeed, the primary activity of humankind is faith. Regardless of whether one claims to be religious or devoutly irreligious, all individuals live by faith. No other explanation exists for anyone getting out of bed every morning except for possessing the confident belief in the truth of an idea, even if this idea is merely making it through another day just to go back to bed. The question is not whether individuals have faith, but rather by what authority do they justify their faith. This justification uses one of four tools.

Some men turn to human reason to justify their getting out of bed in the morning. The discipline that explores human reason and logic is *philosophy*. However, the greatest limitation to philosophy is its inability to prove whether anything is true or false. Philosophy relies on logic, which is able to determine the validity of an argument but not the truth of its conclusion. For example, if a premise is "All men are basically good" and another premise is "John is a man," then the logical conclusion is "John is basically good." The argument is valid, but the conclusion could be either true or false, depending on whether the premises are true or false. Also, questions such as "Is God able to create a rock so heavy that He cannot lift it?" only suggest that the human mind can ask questions that poor reason is incapable of answering. Philosophy is a very poor instrument for justifying one's faith.

Yet there are some self-reliant folks who have suspected reason to be an unreliable guide and who choose to search deep within their beings, hoping that intuition will give the justification that they seek. The reliance upon intuition is called *transcendentalism*. Espoused by Ralph Waldo Emerson, transcendentalism is extremely self-centered and subjective. To find any objective standards by which to guide one's actions is impossible. Emerson's

1. Goals: Substance and Evidence of Pure Education

essay "Self-Reliance" explains that "the great man is he who in the midst of the crowd keeps with perfect sweetness the independence of solitude." Therefore, according to Emerson, a self-imposed alienation is a good thing. However, the society of other people, particularly the family, is required, because goals are only formulated by living and working together. Isolated hermits, like most modern teenagers in their rooms, do not achieve goals. Therefore, a philosophy that will not enrich others is senseless, because values and beliefs must be explicit and obtainable. Anyone who has only intuition, which relies on fickle human emotions, should receive as much pity as Oedipus, who in a moment of intuitional passion, gouged out his own eyes with the golden pins found on his dead wife, who in a moment of intuitional passion hung herself.

On the other hand, many individuals insist that both the human mind and emotions are flawed, declaring that divine revelation gives rise to faith, and God's Word therefore justifies faith. Indeed, since the emotions are fickle, and since the human mind is incapable of answering many questions, divine revelation is absolutely essential for learning about God and man's need for divine reconciliation. Of course, the study of divine revelation is *theology*. Divine revelation is superior over philosophy and transcendentalism because it is objective and is not dependent upon human reason or emotion.

But the issue regarding this objective standard is whether the revelation is authentic and reliable. Which revelation should be followed? For the Christian, the answer is the Bible. However, a Muslim would disagree, claiming the Koran to be authoritative. The Christian must prove to the Muslim that the Bible is superior to the Koran, and vice versa. Yet even among Christians, conflicts over doctrine from or interpretation of the Scriptures indicate that Christians as a community have failed to reach any consensus for over two thousand years. Even though objective truth exists, no one could find it simply by listening to the typical sermon expressed from the modern American pulpit. In short, most Christians have fallen into subjectivity regarding divine revelation and doctrines, relying upon their own opinions, and thus becoming the final authority for their faith and practice. Because of this subjectivity, American Christians are just as lost in the thick fog as any philosopher or transcendentalist when justification of their faith is concerned.

The disciplines of philosophy, transcendentalism, and theology prevailed in their times, but today all three must fight to justify their usefulness in current life on account of the ascendancy of the supposed undisputed superiority of induction, or the discipline of *science*. Since unthinking people believe that science, along with its offspring, technology, has all the answers to life, or at least is working toward those answers, science enjoys such a strong presumption that the burden of proof is becoming more difficult to set forth. After all, like theology, science is based upon an objective standard. And unlike philosophy, science can determine to some extent, but not absolutely, what is true or false. Experiments can be repeated with predictable results. Medical science would be dangerous indeed if the results were not so predictable. Therefore, to most Americans grazing with the bewildered herd in the fog, science seems to be the best way to justify their faith in humankind and the world. To become respectable, one merely needs to attach science to one's discipline, such as "political science," "social science," "library science," or "military science." Actually, some theorists about war still argue that killing fellow human beings is an art, rather than a science. But the results are the same.

With rampant industrialism in the United States, science has been given greater emphasis in the schools, along with increased spending for computers and laboratory equipment. Colleges compete for governmental and corporate grants involving big bucks in order to conduct "scientific studies," which range from anthropology to zoology. And perhaps the greatest fraud of all is the continuation of the National Aeronautical and Space Administration (NASA), which bilks American taxpayers of billions of dollars annually in order to provide jobs for the nation's surplus of scientists.

In spite of the exuberance expressed by scientists, educators, and guinea pigs, science has severe limitations. First of all, science can only demonstrate how things work, and not how things ought to work. In other words, like technical training, science merely transfers processes, not ideas of value. Because they transmit processes about how things work, technical knowledge and scientific know-how are not the same as a culture, which is laden with values.

Also, only physical reality is in the domain of science; values such as truth, justice, and fairness are outside of its realm. Science can split atoms, but only human values can determine whether to use the technology to provide electricity to a city or to drop a bomb on the same city. Since this is true, then technology must be handled by people who are capable of knowing what to do morally. Thus, the teaching of moral philosophy becomes important. The severest problem with science is its inability to produce a single idea by which humans may live. Without ideas, students become bewildered and can honestly say, "I don't know." When asked, "What is equality?" technically trained students will become dumbfounded as their eyes set back into their heads, and their minds become obscured by a fog. This blank stare is a symptom of possessing a blank slate.

But as usual, classifications such as philosophy, transcendentalism, theology, and science often suggest that humankind is in a Hobbesian free-for-all. There is very little objectivity prevailing in which individuals can establish even a simple set of standards for justifying their confident brief in the truth of ideas, that is, their faith. Therefore, any standard for justifying one's faith, even in education, seems hopelessly lost in a fog of conflict. The philosopher yells that the mind is the standard. Yet transcendentalists have their gut feelings that the student's soul can passionately choose better than cold, sterile reason can. The Christian insists that surely the heart is much more important than mind and emotion, because the seat of the affections determines the issues of life. Then the scientist proclaims that physical reality and experience are all there is to life and that when the body dies, existence ceases; therefore, enjoy the present day, because life does not get any better than this. But alas! Humankind continues to walk in circles in the fog, hoping not to stub its toe or bust its head. This blindness that Americans possess whenever education is concerned results from a misunderstanding of faith and its nature.

The fight is not faith against reason or science, but it is rather a civil war among four necessary factions that together justify one's faith: the affections, the emotions, the intellect, and the senses. So long as educators insist that one element is superior to the other three, the issue will never be solved. As usual, the Scriptures come

1. Goals: Substance and Evidence of Pure Education

to the rescue of poor human thinking. Thankfully, the Lord Jesus Christ declares not only the purpose of life but the goal of education as well. The Lord points out that even though they are separate, the heart, the soul, the mind, and the strength are to be subsumed into the godly attribute of *love*. Thus, Mark 12:29–30 states, "And Jesus answered him, The first of all the commandments is, Hear, O Israel; The Lord our God is one Lord: And thou shalt love the Lord thy God with all thy heart, and with all thy soul, and with all thy mind, and with all thy strength: this is the first commandment."

Thus, the civil war comes to an end when all of the different factions bow before God, not because of duty but because of love. The goal of pure education is then the guiding of students to exercise all of their faculties toward loving God. This goal is the substance of the student's faith, which is hoped for above all else. The means for achieving this goal is through a curriculum that exercises the heart, the soul, the mind, and the senses of the student. Students who are capable of loving God are able to govern themselves well. In fact, self-governed citizens under God require no group of social planners to direct their lives. However, faith always has two parts: first, the substance of things hoped for, and second, the evidence of things not seen.

Educators greatly err if they think that their students can learn to love God in isolation. Indeed, faith must be demonstrated, and society is required for achieving the student's goal. In his book *Leviathan*, Thomas Hobbes states that by applying the golden rule, men will leave their state of war, an absolute melee, which makes life "solitary, poor, nasty, brutish, and short." If one wishes to live a long life, then a respect toward the lives of others is absolutely necessary. If individuals desire to be secure in their possessions, then they must allow others to enjoy their possessions. Of course, the assumption that Hobbes makes is that people are reasonable as well as selfish characters.

However, whether they are reasonable or not, the Lord Jesus Christ states that individuals are social creatures and require the company of others in order to show their love for God. Concerning this point, the Lord reminded his hearers of the following commandment: "And the second is like, namely this, Thou shalt love thy neighbour as thyself. There is none other commandment greater than these" (Mark 12:31). Regarding pure education, this commandment reveals three points. First, students loving their God is equal to their loving their neighbors, which is the evidence of the unseen substance of faith. Second, students are to love their neighbors, not humankind. A neighbor is specific and concrete; humankind is general and abstract. Students will show no love by having a burden for the "poor"; on the other hand, they will demonstrate love by taking a bag of groceries to their next-door neighbor who is out of work. Perhaps the poor are always with us because the poor exist in our minds, not in houses. And third, students must love themselves first before they can love their neighbors. Students must enrich themselves first in order to have the capacity to enrich others. Therefore, pure education determines whether the student achieves the goal of loving God by examining how well the student enriches others, not by testing how much the student knows about specific material in a particular discipline.

Since the substance of the goal is simply hoped for and cannot be physically proven, it becomes necessary that the student's love of God must be manifested through the tangible evidence of the

1. Goals: Substance and Evidence of Pure Education

enrichment of neighbors. Students who state that they love God yet cannot seem to get along with their parents, their siblings, or their neighbors are living a lie. Therefore, a student's conduct in life shows whether the student has a central core of convictions or not. In addition to this, implied with loving one's neighbor is a love for the culture in which the neighbor resides. Neighbors who work and live together develop worthwhile values that are shared. In that God must be accepted by faith, which is unseen, believers cannot seclude themselves apart from others; otherwise, the exercising of faith is dead; or in other words, the believer has no goals, or ultimate values.

Therefore, pure education cultivates students by leading them to govern themselves well, bringing heart, soul, mind, and strength under the control of the Holy Spirit. These faculties of the whole person are exercised through the curriculum, not in a utilitarian manner, but as an end in itself. Daily the student is tested to show evidence of a love for God by demonstrating a love for neighbors, which includes parents and siblings. If students are dishonest, unjust, impure, and unlovely to their neighbors, then a love for God, even though it is professed, becomes doubtful. In addition to having students govern themselves, pure education nurtures ladies and gentlemen, who must value themselves as special creations with unique purpose before they can love others. Only then can these ladies and gentlemen extend to their worthy neighbors the qualities of kindness, understanding, and generosity. This evidence of the unseen love for God permits the student to step out of the fog and into the realms of day, the culmination of faith.

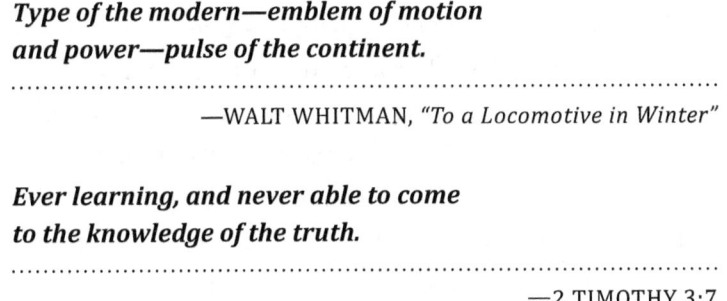

FOUNDATIONS
American Schools and Industrialism

*Type of the modern—emblem of motion
and power—pulse of the continent.*

—WALT WHITMAN, *"To a Locomotive in Winter"*

*Ever learning, and never able to come
to the knowledge of the truth.*

—2 TIMOTHY 3:7

If public education has a foundation, one would have a difficult time trying to discover the basis for it from the educational philosophers—even if every book in print were read regarding the philosophy of education. Oddly, both state and private colleges offer "foundations" as an upper-level course to their education students. Yet how can one build a suitable structure without first working on a solid foundation? In their literature, the educationalists usually offer four foundations for education, which appeal to history, philosophy, psychology, or sociology. Of course, the squabbling over which foundation reigns supreme is all very entertaining, but like the cat chasing its felid tail, the discussion expends a tremendous amount of energy in order to go nowhere. This merry display of pooled ignorance exists because the accepted educational foundations are artificial and are subject to a major limitation inherent with all humans: the limitation of subjective judgment. None of these so-called foundations are objective, because they depend upon the human mind and require some interpretation. Even though educationalists insist on extolling the virtues of unregenerate human reason, anyone who reads a newspaper is reminded daily that all that human reason has produced in the world for the past four thousand years amounts to a lot of misery, oppression, and death. Therefore, instead of praising human reason, educationalists ought to pity it. To ask reason to provide a solid foundation for education is like expecting a bottomless bucket to bail water from a sinking ship. We cannot expect imperfect human reason to perform something it simply is incapable of doing.

But to suppose that the public schools have no foundation at all is to suppose incorrectly. Educational foundations are difficult to discern, because foundations are hidden from view. Therefore, the Christian community has been wonderfully misled by its spiritual, educational, and philosophical leaders. Many Christians continue to believe erroneously that the foundation making the public schools so evil is secular humanism, because the philosophers asserted that education is religious by nature. Yet this assertion is wrong: education is **familial** by nature. Therefore, Christian philosophers are incorrect whenever they glibly suggest that American schools can be cured by allowing God, prayer, and the Bible back into the classrooms. Also, just as wrong is the political belief that if enough

2. Foundations: American Schools and Industrialism

Christian politicians could get elected to public school boards, then the supposed foundation of humanism, if not joyfully replaced with a Christian foundation, would be at least neutralized.

Nevertheless, many Christian parents rejected the political solution and thought the better course of action would be to separate from the public institutions of learning by establishing Christian schools. Even though separation from the governmental schools is certainly a step in the right direction, Christians, who believed that humanism was the enemy, greatly mistook the actual foundation for the public schools. But as they set out to overtake the godless, humanistic schools by hoping to enroll a larger number of students, the Christian schools were doomed to failure.

This certain destruction resulted from sincere Christians believing that a sufficient foundation for education could be realized if a godly curriculum and the Bible usurped the foundation of humanism. But unfortunately, the false foundation remained, which was merely masked by lofty, pious statements of faith. Shortly, most Christian students (although one doubts whether the majority were ever born-again) became worldly, became careless in spiritual matters, and demonstrated a positive contempt for the Bible. If the word *Christian* were not attached to the name of the schools, few of these "hotbeds for the Lord" would be distinguishable from the public schools today.

Fortunately, some Christian parents began to realize the hazardous condition of Christian schools, even though these parents incorrectly believed the schools' educational foundation to be strong. Discerning parents knew that the Christian schools were plagued with the same problems as the public institutions: worldliness, wrong kind of peer pressure, and poor teacher interaction with students. Today, any advantage of sending children to a Christian school seems no longer compelling. While the Christian school may appear to produce brighter students in the elementary grades, eventually the intelligence of both public and Christian high school graduates become about the same. Not only this, but students in the Christian schools dress like public school students, enjoy modern music like public school students, and have the same goal of "getting a good job" like public school students.

If their children were to become educated in physical and spiritual safety, the parents realized that they would have to do the teaching themselves. Parents believed, and rightly so, that they could do a better job with their children at home than the Christian school could. In addition to this, the parents received the added bonus of no longer paying tuition, which merely allowed their children the privilege to learn from their classmates how to cuss and tell dirty jokes.

Finally deciding to teach her children at home, the home educator begins to ponder as all educators have done since Adam tried to instruct Eve concerning God's commandment regarding the tree of knowledge—what is the best way to instruct students, and what materials should be used? While this concern is natural to the teacher, any initial reflection would be more profitable by determining first what should be the foundation of the home school. The answer to this question is paramount before struggling with any other issue concerning the education of children. In that they have accepted the conclusion espoused by Christian philosophers and educators that the public schools are built on humanism and that humanism should be replaced with the Bible, home educators have failed to reflect much upon this vital metaphysical point.

2. Foundations: American Schools and Industrialism

However, while Christians established schools in the 1970s largely because of humanism, racial integration, or poor quality in the public schools, home educators, on the other hand, have reacted generally both to the worldliness in the Christian schools and only recently to the violence and the mismanagement of COVID-19 in the public schools. Regrettably, for this latter reason, many newcomers to home education are *crisis*, rather than committed, educators. Even so, parents are absolutely right to withdraw their children from spiritual and physical dangers; however, reacting to problems fails to offer solid foundations for meaningful education. Because they have toted the miseducational baggage first from the public and then from the Christian schools at the beginning of their pedagogical journey, it is no small wonder that home educators tend to worry about whether their children will secure a good job or be able to compete in the global marketplace. Even though home educators may instinctively see the ultimate goal of education as producing students who can govern themselves well, most parents have built their schools upon the wrong foundation. In short, the goal for the journey is correct; the foundation for the journey is sadly incorrect. Therefore, the first task at hand is to uncover the foundation of public education, which will also reveal the footing upon which Christian education has borrowed only to its own detriment.

If the foundation for public education is not human reason or secular humanism, then what is it? Ever since the Puritans first arrived in New England and established their village schools, mass-production—or *industrialism*—has asserted itself as the actual foundation upon which American tax-supported education rests. Before 1642, the Massachusetts Bay Colony charged fathers and masters to instruct their sons and apprentices respectively in reading. Of course, according to the leaders of the theocracy, reading the Bible was essential for learning more about God. However, the magistrates suspected that parents and masters were negligent in their duties, and local selectmen were tasked to randomly examine any boy regarding his reading and his knowledge of both church doctrine and civil laws. If the poor lad was deemed deficient in the above outcomes, the father or master was fined. Later, true to form of all governments, which create problems only to offer the solution of more government, the Puritan leaders were convinced that an appalling number of children had learning deficiencies, which prompted the passing of the "Old Deluder Satan Act." This law was the first in the New World to require the delightful coercion of "children" (interpreted by most villages to include only boys) to go to school. Another provision in the law allowed the magistrates to take a young boy from his parents when, according to the leaders' august wisdom, the parents were remiss in their educational duties, and to assign the mentally malnourished tyke to a master so that the boy could learn a trade. Needless to say, this provision put a chilling effect upon any home education. Since the communities were small, and the distance to the school was conducive to a leisurely stroll that was suitable for foot-dragging boys, the imposition to families and students was minimal.

However, the purpose for this universal education was not to ensure the salvation of the youth, or to develop the minds of individual students, but to preserve the nature of the Puritan theocracy. In other words, the church-state wanted to mass-produce its own brand of citizens for the continuance of the theocracy, believing that parents were poor instructors for the aims of the Puritan

2. Foundations: American Schools and Industrialism

society. The law of the land was administered haphazardly by different villages and towns, which interpreted the pronouncement in multifarious ways. Indeed, some towns believed that "children" in the law included, oddly enough, girls as well as boys; so these citizens journeyed to a brave, new world by educating the fairer sex. Yet many more towns never bothered to establish a school, making the law of no effect. At the heart of this resistance was the dislike for compulsory education, regardless of the sagacious reasons for its benign demand. To usurp a legitimate role of the family is tyrannical regardless of whether the tyrant is the church or the state—or both.

Later, as years went by, some Puritan farmers decided to trade their plows for stills. Conventional wisdom at the time rumored that running a distillery was easier and more profitable than farming. After all, a farm produces only food; a still produces lots of money. Rum became the cash "crop" of New England, because Africa developed a thirst for alcohol. In exchange for the rum, the New England ships, some of the best in the world, were loaded with African slaves to be sold in the Indies and the Southern colonies. The Puritan theocracy began to grow weak as its merchants began to grow wealthy. With his excess funds, the merchant speculated financially on lands to the West. The small farmer had to buy the land at inflated prices from the merchant, borrowing money for equipment from the merchant's bank, only to lose everything whenever nature frowned unfavorably upon him. With a steady increase in wealth, the New England merchant became politically powerful as well. The gospel of success was proclaimed across New England, with private schools leading the way. Advertisements announced how young men could become a success in life through mathematics, navigation, surveying, gunnery, and even building forts. The underlying ethos of New England changed from a clergy-dominated society to a merchant-driven one. The educators dropped the need for studies in Latin and Greek by adopting courses toward successful money-making and by pushing vocational training, until the War between the States began.

The principal issue behind the war was whether a state, which entered into a voluntary federation, could peacefully leave said federation. The North said "no"; the South said "yes." But to prove that the Southerners were mistaken, the Yankees mobilized an army backed by industrial might and went South for several winters until 1877, ensuring the misguided South was sufficiently reconstructed of her erring ways.

However, underlying the conflict were two competing ways of life as well. The North became progressive, always going forward; the South was conservative, always sustaining a culture. The North sought and got money from the federal government to improve the Northern citizens' self-esteem with roads, canals, and railroads. The South asked for nothing from the federal government, except to be left alone. Yet because of its agricultural products, the South contributed to the U.S. Treasury more than 75 percent of the federal government's income. Therefore, the North benefited at the expense of the South. Indeed, the Northern industries were strengthened wondrously during the war, while the Southern agricultural economy was crippled badly, well-nigh unto death.

With the end of the war, Northern teachers went into high gear by training immigrants in the common schools up North to be progress-loving citizens and by teaching ex-slaves in the Freedmen's schools down South to be loyal and Southern-hating Repub-

2. Foundations: American Schools and Industrialism

licans. Later, most states mandated compulsory education under the guise of educating the youth of America. But instead of educating the minds of the youth, the teachers preached the gospel of progress throughout the land. This mass optimism for endless progress created large-scale businesses, which had an inordinate reliance upon machines. Since these large economies of scale result in the overproduction of goods, mass advertising and a formidable army of marketers were now required to move the product, which is accomplished by enticing consumers to lust after a product that they do not need. When the novelty of any product disappears, the industrialists introduce "new and improved" models to replace the perfectly good products just recently purchased. In order to purchase all of this unnecessary stuff, consumer credit became necessary, thus enslaving the consumer completely to finance companies and banks. Nevertheless, if this rampant consumerism were the only evil with industrialism, then perhaps Americans could sleep well at night in spite of their migraines, ulcers, and insomnia. But the greatest wickedness regarding industrialism is the destruction of the souls of both individuals and their nation.

Industrialism has a voracious appetite for natural resources, labor, and capital. Not working in harmony with nature, industrialism tries to conquer and control the land and other natural elements. To ensure a continuous supply of workers, public educators must indoctrinate the student first in the glory of global progress, and second in the necessity of making a good living and of "fitting into American society." Therefore, like the New England schools before the War between the States, at the heart of public education is mass production with an eye toward vocational training, which attempts to prepare students to take their place in the job market.

Indeed, so long as students can successfully fill out a tax form, their training is apparently complete. Yet in spite of the utopian promises that working hard will have its rewards, the gullible student fails to find either a good job or even a good living and despairs absolutely for the good life. Instead of finding the American dream, the common high school graduate receives a nightmare, complete with alienation, frustration, and finally, a miserable death.

Industrialism does not deal with human beings. What used to be the "personnel office" has been replaced with the "department of human resources." Relationships between owner and worker are often impersonal, with no lasting bonds created. Workers do no more work than is required, and owners do not feel any obligation to their human resources once they have handed the resources their paychecks. Graded-classroom instruction displays much of this impersonality between teachers and students, where genuine affections are seldom developed. Long-distance satellite and Internet instruction only compounds the lack of personal affection and physical contact. While labor-saving devices may be created, rarely do the devices ease the work of the laborer. If anything, the new marvelous contrivance puts the worker out into the street to find another job. If the displaced "human resources" can read the help-wanted section in the newspaper, they may feel obliged to thank a teacher. But thanks aside, the typical worker fails to be secure. Due to the industrial cycles of boom and bust, at any point in time millions of workers are unemployed, and those who give up looking for a good job create a class of paupers, living in poverty. All of this is done in the name of competition and progress, which has no end, no goal, and no meaning.

2. Foundations: American Schools and Industrialism

Therefore, industrialism creates a restless, moving mass of "human resources," which does not know where it is heading. When a society is always in flux, the idea of a culture is meaningless. The very word *culture* connotes stability and security, requiring nurturing like a garden requires cultivating. However, industrialism is neither stable nor secure, and it cannot be self-sufficient. Indeed, industrialism is not merely incapable of having a culture but is also *anti-cultural*, actively working against any culture.

The industrialized nation must be sustained with the weakening of agrarian communities and small towns by displacing men and women from their roots and by putting them to work in the nation's factories, offices, or military. A large military is necessary, because industrialism must have wars in order to progress. Whether a world war, a simple police action, or a peacekeeping mission, industrial might must have new markets in order to sell its inevitable overproduction. Since killing and dying is an unwholesome occupation, the industrialized nation must conscript its "acceptable losses" from among its citizens, who instinctively believe that dying is not much of a life. But this carnage is justified and tolerated as long as worldwide democracy and progress ever moves forward.

Worse even than this bloodshed, Americans tolerate the mass production of their children into model citizens for the new world order, becoming ready to face the challenges of the new global economy. While they are equipped to push buttons, American students are void of ideas when they enter the college classroom. Regardless of whether they are trying to teach a good philosophy or a bad one, college professors are becoming more distressed with their students, because the most common answer in the classroom is "I don't know." But public education was not designed to prepare students for college. Since most students successfully find some sort of job, American public education is not a failure; indeed, the system has been very successful by using industrialism as its foundation. So why should anyone be upset if America lags behind other nations in test scores, the educational foundations of which are not linked to industrialism and everlasting progress? Only in the United States is progress an obsession. In a mass-produced economy, perfection is not expected. Therefore, so long as the products from the public schools perform the task of dehumanized labor, Americans ought to be gratified that their school system has produced the maximum amount of mediocrity for the greatest number of future human resources.

In short, industrialism is artificial, an aberration of nature, a parasite that destroys culture by sucking the life out of nature and humans. Progress is not a good in itself. Yet Americans accept it as such. What is the destination of progress, and what are its goals? Both of these common-sense inquiries cannot be answered absolutely. Herein rests the fallacy under which the Christian school labors. Not only did the schools adopt the mass-production model of public schools by herding students into graded classrooms, but also, by misunderstanding the true foundation of the public schools, Christians had adopted industrialism as the foundation for their own brand of training. While the goal may be defined as teaching students to govern themselves well under God, the school's foundation is sabotaging the results. No doubt, Christian teachers will raise a unified cry that their schools are founded upon the Bible. However, these noble souls are sadly deceived. How can students learn to love God when their souls are lusting for material

2. Foundations: American Schools and Industrialism

goods and for a good money-making job in order to get ahead in the world? For an example, as part of its English curriculum, one Christian publisher has twelfth-grade students write a research paper about the job they wish to pursue after graduation. Apparently, the publisher does not think that attending college is an option, or if students do go to college, they are merely extending their vocational training a few more years. Hundreds of Christian schools use this curriculum, and yet the principals and teachers would insist that their particular school honors God and His Word.

To casually ask these schools to produce all papers that were written by their female students who researched the job of housewife and mother would undoubtedly produce only a lot of knitted brows and embarrassed looks. How can these schools produce any such research papers when girls, who are mixed with boys, must compete with the boys for grades, class standing, and teachers' affection? This competition is a strange way to teach girls to be obedient to their future husbands. It is no small wonder that so many young ladies dislike being women, since they are taught to be competitive in school and in the future job market. If the Christian school segregated its students by gender, then perhaps the situation would improve, but only if the boys learn leadership and the girls learn submission. Yet this simple, straightforward biblical truth will be ignored on account of a lack of teachers and impracticability; that is, political incorrectness.

But this is not all. Regardless of "grade checks" at most Christian schools, the excellence of spiritual and intellectual pursuits is secondary to the spirit of money-making sports. Often, students must travel long distances to play their opponents (who cease to be fellow Christian brothers and sisters); therefore, team members are dismissed early from classes with the blessings of the principal, who prays that the school's team will beat the other team. A victory would give the school bragging rights and may attract more "talented" students to the school.

In addition to this, in both small and large schools, this mass exodus of warriors decimates classes such that any instruction to any remaining non-warriors becomes ridiculous. This going forth to battle against these hateful foes is all done in the name of Christ and competition. Fights have even broken out between students—and parents—from the different Christian schools. The greatest pressure upon Christian schools to pursue sport programs comes from the parents of the students. After all, who will ever make a million dollars contemplating metaphysics, Hobbes's state of war, Latin, or the second coming of Christ? On the other hand, sport training brings lots of money into the school's coffers and gives young men and women the opportunity to perfect their skills in order to apply for sport scholarships at colleges and a chance for a job with the big leagues, where millions of dollars can be had. So long as the Christian school insists on clinging to industrialism as its foundation, its students will never know God, much less even learn to enjoy Him. For the hundreds of Christian schools to give up their industrialism will require either a supernatural moving of God upon the hearts of the principals, teachers, parents, and students, or the schools' eventual bankruptcy, either spiritually, financially, or both.

Therefore, in view of the above discussion, if parents wish their students to be able to govern themselves and to experience the good life, not a mythical good living, then the home school ought

2. Foundations: American Schools and Industrialism

to avoid by all means possible the false educational foundation adopted by the public and Christian schools. Industrialism, along with its demi-gods progress and competition, must be torn up and repudiated completely if pure education is to have any eternal value at all. Fortunately, if it is operating under industrialism due to ignorance, the home school can easily correct the problem. The home school enjoys a flexibility not shared by many Christian schools. In that the foundation of both public and Christian schools has now been exposed after removing the debris of the broken and crumbled souls of students, home educators can now turn to the task of learning the nature of the proper foundation for their schools.

03 FOUNDATIONS
The Home School and Independence

Thus dwelt together in love these simple Acadian farmers,—
Dwelt in the love of God and of man.
Alike were they free from
Fear, that reigns with the tyrant, and envy, the vice of republics.

—HENRY WADSWORTH LONGFELLOW, "Evangeline"

And the chief captain answered, With a great sum obtained I this freedom. And Paul said, But I was free born.

—ACTS 22:28

The love of money is the heartbeat of industrialism, the foundation for all governmental schools and for the better part of all private schools. On the other hand, the love for a purposeful life for its students ought to be the lifeblood of the home school. For the lack of a better term, this love for a purposeful life is called *culturalism*. In the context of this chapter and the rest of this book, the term *culturalism* means the natural human desire to enjoy personal independence with self-responsibility and to establish a permanent legacy through a fulfilling life that is worthy to be transmitted to the next generation. If these desires dwell not within the human heart, then having children becomes a meaningless, silly joke. But bringing children into the world is no joking matter. The only human institution capable of nurturing and fulfilling the desires for meaningful freedom and stability is the family. Like the anchor preventing a ship from endless drifting, the family should offer every generation of children a reliable stay to prevent self-destruction and despair. Yet modern America may be remembered well in history as producing the most callous parents, because mothers and fathers refused to take personal responsibility for the welfare of their own children.

Industrialism, with its love for money, produces only evil; culturalism, with its love for freedom, produces a harmony with nature and a reliance on nature's God, which leads to contentment, or in other words, a purposeful life. Thus, culturalism strengthens the family, while industrialism destroys it. Because this is true, by inciting lust and greed, the man-made common school is both morally and economically wrong; on the other hand, the home school arises naturally from the primary moral and economic bond in society—the family. Therefore, by opposing industrialism, with its endless progress toward alienation and death, the home school offers a way to reconciliation and life.

Interestingly, because it sympathizes with a life of purpose, culturalism harmonizes well with the tenets of agrarianism. To understand what agrarianism is, we must begin by understanding perfectly what it is not. First, agrarianism is not a hostility toward machines and factories. Small, local factories with current technol-

3. Foundations: The Home School and Independence

ogy are good for any society. What agrarians do oppose are centralized megacorporations monopolizing a nation's resources purely for financial gain, and not for efficient production of goods and services. History demonstrates that centralized bigness is not necessarily better.

Second, agrarianism is not a plan to force millions of urbanites to begin farming in the country. Because the honorable livelihood of small-scale farming has been maligned by the industrialists in politics, economics, and education, the masses in recent years have never believed farming to be a viable vocation. However, if agriculture were treated fairly, then no doubt more citizens would at least consider the advantages of this way of life.

And third, agrarianism is not an acceptance of a lower standard of living or quality of life. However, agrarians reject the myth that an increased standard of living results only from everlasting progress. Financial markets and overproduction of unnecessary goods is not wealth. True wealth resides in productive land and within the soul and mind of every individual. Whether one lives in the city or in the country, agrarianism is a way of thinking, first, and a way of life, second.

Agrarianism, then, emphasizes a love for self-sufficiency and desires working in harmony with nature. Therefore, the connection between culturalism, agrarianism, the home school, and pure education becomes apparent. The home school harmonizes with nature, because education is the natural prerogative of the family. Thus, unlike the public schools' artificial foundation of industrialism, the home school enjoys an objective foundation that is cultural, which is connected to the land itself. If the educational foundation is industrialism, then the schools train future workers. On the other hand, if the educational foundation is culturalism, then the schools educate future leaders. Pure education is about securing freedom to obtain ideas, not about conquering processes to obtain a job. The only schools capable of doing any serious educating in the United States, then, are the home schools.

Whether urban or rural, every family has a school. Some of these schools are well-defined, while in other homes, the parents do not consciously think of themselves as having a school. Yet no one can deny that learning and instruction take place every day of the year in every family, with lessons being taught and learned, with tests being given, and with rewards or punishments being meted out. From the moment that Adam and Eve entered into a mutual compact in Eden to set up a household under God, a whole lot of learning began to take place. Since the days of our first ancestors, husbands and wives have instructed each other for good or for ill. The first cry of the baby brings a whole new reason for the school's existence. When not listening to veteran parents about the best way to approach parenthood, new moms and dads read everything about how to care for their future hopes, which are embodied in a fragile child. These helpless beings are nurtured and protected by the mother, who teaches self-reliance and language to her tots in such a way to cause a philosopher to only speculate endlessly. Indeed, very young children learn the basics of ethics, religion, economics, communication, and personal care from their parents, and they experience love, security, and self-worth by observing their parents interact with each other. At least, this is the ideal. The household that does not value honest work, intellectual leisure, or cultural stability will still teach and instruct, but the

3. Foundations: The Home School and Independence

course offerings in theft, laziness, and turmoil are detrimental to the family's very existence.

Oddly, after this initial—and for the most part, successful—training of young children, parents are all too ready to kick their children out of the home school whenever children become "old enough to go to school." But then, maybe the verb *kicked out* gives the wrong idea, because the parents are coerced by threats and with humiliation into doing the booting. Students skip off to the educational factories, not because they are motivated by some latent virtue common to all young scholars but because the technocrats kindly insist that they leave the security of their families in order to socialize with other similarly displaced children. Since the students are corralled by their teachers, who state repeatedly that they are free, these "future leaders of America" are held hostage in an abnormal setting for at least ten or more years. This makes for a strange lesson in liberty, when freedom has to be taught in a walled cell with marker boards next to several other inmates, and where outside the room, armed guards, sheriffs, or police officers patrol the halls. But according to the government, parents have to be forced to have their children trained; otherwise, the youngsters would never know that they were free citizens in the freest nation on earth.

This coerced liberty arose during the 1800s, when state officials discovered that when the common schools had voluntary attendance, absenteeism among the youthful volunteers was high—as much as 50 percent on any given day. While Southern children met occasionally in "old-field schools," where the rudiments of reading and writing were learned, the schools were generally private with modest tuition. These schools met sporadically, adjusting themselves to nature's time clock of planting and reaping, not to the arbitrary caprice of bureaucrats. On the other hand, most children in the North went to school haphazardly because they had to work in the factories, which ignored all seasons. The work was hard, the hours were long, and the pay was pitiful. One pittance did not provide much, but when pooled with the other household pittances, the industrialized family who worked together stayed together—at least economically.

With the rise of labor unions, the compassionate cry from the brotherhoods for compulsory education dinned steadily upon the ears of the state and national politicians, who finally decided this policy was truly a wise one. Of course, unofficially the fact that the politicians accepted a lot of union money for their campaigns and retirement funds had nothing to do with this decision. While teaching children to read and write is noble and just, the actual motive was the labor unions' wanting to rid factories and mines of cheap child labor and thus command higher wages for the adults. Today, in that attendance is mandated by law, parents have no choice but to make their children attend some sort of school. Since government schools appear to be more gentle to the laborer's paycheck, public education remains the solid choice of free people in "the land of the free, and the home of the brave."

Yet even though public officials, with a myriad of professional educators, resist the trend, parents are declaring their independence from the government and taking the responsibility to teach their own children again. These students are "privately tutored," which connotes a privilege of the well-to-do and a superior method of learning due to its excellent student-teacher ratio. Although increasingly more children are experiencing daycare as a substi-

3. Foundations: The Home School and Independence

tute for mother because "mommy has to work," most children still enjoy being privately tutored at home for several years before they are shuttled off to their benign prisons. Thankfully, due to the maternal instinct of protecting their young, an increasing number of women, with the cooperation of their husbands, are continuing to tutor their children in the privacy of their homes, even up through high school. By removing their children from danger, parents have become independent from the government and have reclaimed a large part of their sovereignty by educating at home. So far, the secessionist movement begun by home educators has met limited opposition from the educational bureaucrats. The minimal resistance is due to the politicians still recognizing the sovereignty of parents over their own children. But as more families reclaim their right to educate their children, resistance should increase, because now significant sums of money will be taken away from the school systems. Money is always the central issue concerning those who control monopolies, public or private.

Culturalism asserts an independence that is just as important to the home educator as to the tiller of the soil. The yeoman farmer works hard to cultivate a garden, to plant and harvest a cash crop, and to keep the farm in good repair. If he fails after giving the soil his best effort, then the farmer knows that no one is to blame but himself. The rhythm of the rural life is seldom hurried, moving with nature's seasons. The self-sufficient farmer is truly a free man, who breathes the air of liberty and self-responsibility. In like manner, the home educator is free, allowed to work with nature. One student may excel in a subject, so adjustment in the curriculum is necessary, ensuring the student is sufficiently challenged. Another student may struggle with the same subject; here a slower pace is advisable so that the student avoids frustration. Yet the slower pace does not disturb the flow of learning for either student. The home educator instructs each student as a special individual with unique talents, not as the mythological average pupil, who must catch up or be left behind. If, after working conscientiously with their students, failure should result in the venture, then the parents can at least know that they did all that they could do and cannot assign blame to another agency or individual. Hence, the home school enjoys freedom in its finest sense, but it shoulders the responsibility for the results as well.

Embodied in the concept of independence is the idea of decentralization. The home school disproves the myth that bigger is better. The public school can no longer insist that its model for education is efficient. While every year taxpayers pay over $12,000 or more for each public school student, the home school operates on a budget often well below $1,000 per year, and this figure may include several students. In addition to this, the home school does not need to construct a building for its instruction, nor are buses necessary for transportation and for the social-engineering fad currently in vogue. Also, since students outnumber the teachers 25 to 1 (and sometimes the ratio is higher), classroom management in the public school certainly is not more efficient. On the other hand, home educators have an average of three students per teacher. As a result of the better ratio, home school students socialize and communicate better with adults and perform better academically. The reasons for this disparity between the public and home schools center on the public schools being centralized into large inefficient units and the home schools being decentralized into smaller efficient ones.

3. Foundations: The Home School and Independence

This same disparity is true with any sphere of human activity, particularly in economics and politics. Megacorporations, which merge together—not for better production, but merely for financial gain—are extremely inefficient and precarious to employees and consumers. Without being loaded down with a heavy overhead, the smaller decentralized company, which uses modern technology, produces better goods at a cheaper cost than the large-scale corporations, which must have a large hierarchy of non-productive upper and middle managers, a large fleet of trucks for transportation, and a huge budget for advertising. The public school is burdened in the same way with a top-heavy bureaucracy, fleets of buses, and advertising for "stay-in-school" and "we're-doing-a-great-job" campaigns. Because home educators are producing superior products with more efficiency, the decentralized home school will continue to be an embarrassment to the supposed governmental monopoly on education. When they are about to go under, the educational industrialists can be expected to whine for congressional help. Like the Chrysler Corporation many years ago, when it whimpered to national politicians that its continued existence was necessary for the good of the nation, so the public schools will suggest the same tripe. The solution for the industrialist will always be more money and more legislation to restrict competition.

Even with nations, bigger is not better. The designers of a worldwide democracy ignore a fundamental lesson from nature: healthy organisms do not grow indefinitely; they grow to a certain point and then naturally divide. If a cell continues to grow, we call this cancer. If there is to be any worldwide state, the democratic union will be ruled by the majority's say-so—not by persuasion, but by force—as history has constantly shown. Regional differences will ensure just about as inharmonious a marriage as one can possibly ever imagine. However, not only do the reconstructionists ignore the natural separation of organisms, but they lack discernment regarding the nature of democracy; that is, any democracy has inherently the seeds for its own destruction. This self-destruction is due to a democracy's having always a majority and a minority, a winner and a loser. Hence, the loser will always try to resist the winner by any means possible. History reveals that whenever two nations, two races, or two opinions co-exist, cooperation is achieved only by one group dominating the other by force. If public education does succeed in reaching its goal of a world democracy, the people's government of the world's citizens will be established by the pointing of guns, not by the cooperation of a tolerant majority and condescending minority. Tyranny by any other name is still tyranny.

Past empires demonstrate these two laws well. The great empires of the past—Babylonian, Persian, Alexandrian, Roman, and British—became so large, the administration became so burdensome, and power became so concentrated that they exploded into smaller units. These past empires also had the august role of being the world's policeman in their times. The last two remaining empires—the United States, the current world's policeman, and China (the next policeman?)—are sure to follow in the ruins of these other abnormal monstrosities of world history. That the United States is in reality an empire of separate countries cannot be denied. For an example, if it were an independent nation, the State of Georgia would rank twenty-sixth in the world, with a Gross National Product of over 626 billion dollars. Georgia would have a larger GNP than nations such as Saudi Arabia, Switzerland, Sweden,

3. Foundations: The Home School and Independence

Egypt, and Belgium. These countries are hardly developing nations. In addition to this, Georgia, with over ten million citizens, would have a larger population than nations such as El Salvador, Costa Rica, Croatia, Denmark, and Finland. In short, Georgia could take its place in the world as an independent, self-sufficient country based on GDP and population alone. California and Texas are in reality massive nation-states. The point here is that since only 536 men and women determine how to spend trillions of dollars a year, this is a lot of power. Since every national representative speaks for over 690,000 constituents, anyone who suggests that the United States is a representative-democracy must be a madman. Indeed, no one should wonder why the national government is so inept. According to the fortunes of previous empires following the course of nature, the United States will downsize either peacefully or violently. But as sure as the former Soviet Union ended in fragments, the United States will downsize as well.

However, the reason why progressivists resist decentralization is because the modern Western tradition is not only materialistic but mechanistic as well. Social engineers arrogantly believe man can establish and change social institutions with planning and science. If society is simply a machine, then bad parts can be removed or overhauled in order to have the social machine working smoothly again. For this reason, having opposition parties in politics is bad, because conflict creates friction. In fact, any friction is undesirable, whether the source is from the individual, the home, or the church. Under the centralized state, compromise is the finest virtue that anyone could possess or develop. The central planners in education would have Americans believe that organization will yield better results if everyone pulls together. However, the only trouble is this: a lot of people refuse to believe the sophistry anymore.

Because the educational bureaucracy has become unresponsive to families, the breaking away from the public schools through private academies and through the Christian and home school movements was naturally inevitable. However, as more parents freely choose to educate their children at home, the Christian and public schools will find themselves with few options. First of all, most Christian schools will become more inefficient than they are now, because inside and outside pressures will demand more vocational training, particularly with computers, business management courses, and sports. Increased tuition will drive more Christian parents toward home education; enrollment will fall, and many schools will go out of business.

On the other hand, the few schools that resist industrialism will do so only by following the model of the antebellum Southern academy, which prepared students for college, not for jobs, and by rejecting the common school model, which prepared students "to take their place in American society." As many have already discovered, the Christian school cannot be all things to all people without disastrous results. The former educational model will mean providing separate classes for boys and girls, dropping interscholastic sport programs, de-emphasizing science, and avoiding business courses such as business math, office management, and computer science. If the student refuses to learn Latin, to read literature, and to exercise rhetoric, then the student needs to go to a vocational school and not waste the Christian educator's time. This transformation will not be easy for the schools, but people of Christian integrity can do it.

3. Foundations: The Home School and Independence

Unfortunately, the public schools will be forced to take action in only one way. When public schools become unable to compete with home schools, whether measured by efficiency or by quality, public educators will become increasingly hostile toward home educators. Since their focus is centered on money and centralization, educational bureaucrats become lugubrious when losing large sums of money, because their enrollments lack the head count of students in private and home schools. Sadly, even some Christian administrators show a bitterness toward home educators, who draw from the pool of Christian students. In short, fewer students mean less money. The public schools' hostility will be transformed into positive oppression using the same avenue traveled by big businesses, which oppress the small factories not by competition but through legislation. Since home schools are decentralized, "big education" will think that it will get its way. But even though they are independent, home educators have a commonality of purpose more powerful than threats and intimidation. Indeed, the public educators, like all money-grabbing industrialists, have more bark than bite, as shown by the sniveling behavior of Chrysler many years ago. These toothless lapdogs will be no match for a determined people who wish to remain free and independent.

Culturalism is the acme of independence. Indeed, the men who loved their freedom, who loved their farms with the soil, developed the body of early American political and economic thought. Upon these ideas the American way of life rests. The vision of the colonial leaders was a land of small, independent gentlemen-farmers, who were self-sufficient and who received the bounty from the soil by entering into a pact that harmonized with nature. These men of the soil were not competitors but were rather joined together by the common bond of *culture*. Thus, whenever independent home educators choose to teach their children, these souls enter into the same bond with their ancestors. These were independent men and women, who held the soil in their hands as free human beings, who realized that this possession was worth defending, even—if need be—by dying. This bond is why home educators have an independence as well as a common unity, which shames even the strongest advocates of so-called diversity.

04 FOUNDATIONS
The Home School and Culture

No race can prosper until it learns there is as much dignity in tilling a field as in writing a poem.

—BOOKER T. WASHINGTON, *1895 Atlanta speech*

One generation passeth away, and another generation cometh: but the earth abideth for ever.

—ECCLESIASTES 1:4

As shown in the previous chapter, a foundation can be defined by its essence, which is an independent base not relying upon the rest of the structure. Even though a building may be torn down completely, the foundation will remain, because the footing is the lowest part, hidden from view. The foundation derives its strength from the solid earth, not from any man-made edifice. With culturalism as its foundation, home education enjoys its independence. Not only do teachers have liberty to teach, but the students have perfect liberty to learn. For this reason, the home educator can ignore all advice offered and the outcomes espoused by the state's educationalists without losing any sleep. A sound sleep is the prerogative of a free individual.

Not only defined by its essence, but a foundation can be defined by its function as well. All foundations support a structure. If the foundation is not sturdy nor solid, then instead of being secure, the building will eventually suffer ruin. Hence, any defect in the foundation will cause damage to the structure. In chapter 2, industrialism was shown to offer neither stability nor security for an educational foundation. If one were to look at the public school edifice, undoubtedly the opinion would be that the structure seems sound, even after 170 years. However, the apparent soundness is not due to the foundation but is the result of damage-control, by which the walls are being supported by lots of money and myths. Governmental teachers play a vital role by hard selling to millions of American students the glory called American progress. However, the cost for this glory has been continual wars, increasing pauperism, and eroding moral strength.

Since both public and Christian schools have industrialism as their foundations, the results are disturbingly the same. Indeed, many Christians have been so disturbed by the sad outcome of their students that they have closed the doors to their schools without reflecting whether the schools were on a bad foundation. This lack of reflection is understandable, in that most Americans assume as an indisputable maxim that progress is a good thing. Obediently, American families continue to provide to the national educational factories an abundance of children, who are the raw material to be groomed to fit into American society. But like any other mass-produced commodity, the young students undergo an impersonal industrial process that fails to generate a unique example of

4. Foundations: The Home School and Culture

fine craftsmanship. The lackluster result is a mediocre product to be employed for the whim of the American elite in industry and government. In a country blessed with abundant and magnificent natural resources, mediocrity among its citizens is not only pathetic but contemptuous as well.

But, for the most part, home educators are not satisfied with mediocre results, and they conscientiously attempt to have their students rise above the bewildered herd of the nation's "human resources." Nevertheless, if their primary concern is centered on ensuring their students will get good jobs or can compete in the global marketplace, then home educators are victims to industrialism as well. If this statement is true, then the home school ceases to be a *home school* and is merely an extension of the public schools. Regardless of whether children are protected both spiritually and physically and even achieves the highest SAT score in the state, if students simply want to get ahead in life to become rich and famous, then they will join the millions of victims who traded their souls for money only to realize that some cosmic joke has been committed against them at their expense. In short, life will not be worth living at all, because the soul will lack inner peace.

If one removes industrialism from underneath the public schools, then the collapse of the schools is certain, because no other meaningful foundation exists to support it. If one removes industrialism from the Christian schools, they may totter a bit; the structure will need to be put on the same foundation as the home schools. Moving a building to a different location and to a different foundation is not easy, but it can be done. If one removes the industrialism from the home school, the school is only strengthened. The real foundation has been holding up the school all along, hidden, unseen, supporting the visible structure.

The reason why the public schools are beyond redemption is because industrialism is the enemy of the family, ensuring the alienation of children from parents, of husbands and wives from each other, and of the entire household from God. The initial understanding of children for orderly society is learned within the context of the family. While a rural family thrives on cooperation among the members of the family to ensure its subsistence, the industrialized family has little common interests because mutual cooperation is unnecessary in a money-based society. Therefore, industrialism encourages the alienation of individuals. Because of this alienation, most marriages will be unhappy unions from the very start. Seldom will the marriage be based on shared spiritual or intellectual values; rather, it will be founded on vague materialistic and physical judgments. Thus, the only solution for the inevitable unhappiness seems to be easy dissolution of the disenchanted in order to try again. However, divorce only compounds the alienation of parents and children. Today, family bonds are viewed primarily as biological, not moral, and duties must be legally enforced, such as in providing child support. With the breakdown of the family and its functions, the logical conclusion asserted by many politicians is that the nation's children belong to the State, not to the parents. However, a foundation that rebels against the family is no foundation at all. With the destruction of the family, the nation falls as well.

On the other hand, the home school restores the purposeful commonality to the family. Even if she has fallen prey to industrialism, the home educator teaches her children, because deep within her soul an instinct prevails. A longing exists within the heart of every sensitive being for something that is lasting, permanent, and

4. Foundations: The Home School and Culture

strong. Every human institution, including the family, needs durability. Instinctively, the home educator knows that teaching is not just a transfer of processes or facts to her children but rather the passing of a rich legacy to the next generation. In his book *Social Institutions*, Joyce O. Hertzler remarks that a family can be called a *home* only when there is a unity in a family having interests in common and a devotion among the members that is mutual. Thus, homes are rare today in the United States. When one considers that many children have their own computer, television, and phones, that fathers retreat into their dens, and that mothers find escape elsewhere, the modern family has become a pool of alienated souls locked away in their own little universes. Thus, going against the trend, the home educator makes a home, and the primary inheritance given to her children is a shared way of life. In his 1886 essay "Sweetness and Light," Matthew Arnold calls this shared way of life "a study of perfection," or in other words, culture.

Like many words in the English language, *culture* is grossly misused. Expressions such as "drug culture" or "pop culture" become nonsensical, because a culture requires unity, stability, and mutuality. Because they are addicted to progress, Americans value novelty over the old, embracing the latest new fad, rather than developing the traditional. Progress is absolutely incapable of providing a culture, because inherent in this constant motion forward is the seed to beget more progress; the latest newness is certain to be replaced with newer technology, newer ideas, and newer whatnots. Donald Davidson, a former professor at Vanderbilt University long ago, points out this lack of culture in his essay "A Mirror for Artists." Because its "human resources" are in constant motion, an industrialized nation must borrow its culture from another source.

Any meaningful art or literature, which imitates nature, disappears, because creative genius is absent.

Twentieth-century American writers and artists produced mostly works of despair and hopelessness. This hopelessness is worse in the twenty-first century. Without artists, paintings no longer grace the walls of homes but are stored in public museums. Without readers, books no longer adorn the shelves of homes but are deposited in public libraries. With urbanization, animals no longer roam the wilds but are caged in public zoos. Sadly, Americans are satisfied with cheaply manufactured copies of the masters and settle for mass-produced novels, magazines, and comic books. In addition to this, modern industrialism completely ignores the best culture of human tradition and borrows from tribal culture, with its pagan music and values expressed with dissonant words and beats and with tattoos and piercing of the body. Instead of attempting to improve personal communications, most Americans are content to stare at their phones.

Also, to even suggest that the empire of the United States has anything approaching an American culture is lunacy. Only a fool would believe that a New England liberal and a Kansas farmer share a way of life marked by unity, mutuality, and stability of purpose. However, several homes with shared ways of life can make a local community, and local communities with shared values and beliefs can create a regional culture. But beyond this limit, any meaningful culture becomes impossible, because ways of life and purpose will conflict between regions. The national elections reveal the enduring division between the industrial North allied with the progressive West coast and the agricultural West and South. Nevertheless, every culture begins with a home. Therefore, the home school must

4. Foundations: The Home School and Culture

transmit a culture in order to be a legitimate home school. Since vocational training and industrialism transfer mere processes and cannot create ideas or values, the home educator must ensure the home school is built squarely on the only foundation possessing stability, solidness, and permanence—the soil.

The vast majority of homes in the United States do not possess much soil. Nevertheless, every home school has some soil to cultivate, even if the only soil is the hearts of the students. Before there can be a love for a nation, there must first be a love for the home; and before there can be a love for the home, there must be a love for the soil. Long before the War for American Independence, men of the soil, not industrialists, developed the ideals of the American republic. According to the founding fathers, a republic can endure only if the citizens are united by similar nationality, language, and religion and only if the division of land is nearly equal. The early gentleman farmers did not compete for markets, nor were they concerned with acquiring lots of money. Working the land was its own reward. John Adams had his Peacefield, George Washington had his Mount Vernon, and Thomas Jefferson had his Monticello.

At the age of one month, Alexander Stephens lost his mother, and at the age of thirteen, he lost his father, who was a teacher and a farmer. As a student, Stephens studied at Franklin College in Athens, Georgia, first to be a minister, but since he had no definite calling from God, he pursued the study of law. Once being admitted to the Georgia Bar, the future vice president of the Confederacy rejected a generous offer to practice law in Columbus in order to go to Crawfordsville, Georgia. This small town in east Georgia had nothing to commend itself to Stephens—except that this was the land where his father had farmed and had died. Stephens's roots were deep in the soil where his father developed a culture. Because he suffered his entire life with illness, Stephens refused to marry, because he did not wish to burden a wife with his frailties. Yet what vexed him the most due to this ill-health was his inability to follow in the footsteps of his father, to be a tiller of the soil. The great men of early America were men of the land, who believed that the tangible soil gave life and freedom, and that this way of life was worthy to be passed on to the next generation of free citizens.

The home school's culturalism is vital not only for the family but for a community's continued existence as well. Yet while the home school tries to preserve and teach worthy values, industrialism wars against tradition, the family, and nature. Tradition is perceived as impeding the advancement of progress, as causing friction, and therefore it must be eliminated. Progressives become frustrated, because tradition lags behind the new and the improved. The family is seen as the depository of bad habits and dangerous ideas, so the industrialized state begins gaining more control of children at a younger age, with K-3 and K-4 tax-supported programs. Whenever vouchers begin to receive widespread support, the government will ensnare those that use the "tickets of choice" by dictating acceptable policy to those who are foolish enough to use the disguised dole. Also, unlike the farmer, who works with nature, industrialists, with their gospel of progress, attempt to conquer and control nature through science. Nevertheless, the home that educates its children is in concord with every home school that has ever existed since ancient times. Indeed, the mutuality of purpose is found even in the question of Hebrew children whenever they inquired of their parents, "What mean ye?"

The Hebrew home school had a three-tiered approach to learning. First, the student would observe the parents performing

4. Foundations: The Home School and Culture

the duties of life. Next, when older, the student would participate in the different ceremonies and occupations of the family. Finally, the student would inquire about the meaning of the duties, ceremonies, and occupations. So, the student watches, then does, and finally asks why. As the father would apply blood across and along the door posts, the child would ask, "What mean ye by this service?" (Exodus 12:26). Here, then, the father is given a rare moment to teach. The father would explain that this ceremony was to commemorate the Passover, when the Lord gave liberty to the Hebrews, freeing them from state oppression, which enslaved them. Even though this service was performed only once a year, the father was commanded to instruct his children daily about the law of God. Again, a teachable moment presented itself whenever the child asked, "What mean the testimonies and the statutes, and the judgments, which the LORD our God hath commanded you?" (Deuteronomy 6:20).

The entire context of the law is the proper conduct of God's people in connection with the integrity of the land and of the home. The child is reminded again that God delivered the Hebrews from slavery, made them free men, and gave them a land to possess. The Hebrew culture, which was bound by the land, would be preserved so long as the commandments of God were obeyed. As the Hebrews crossed the Jordan River, each tribe carried a large stone across to the other side. A monument was built with the twelve stones, and naturally, a child's curiosity would prompt the question, "What mean ye by these stones?" (Joshua 4:6). To this question, the father explained that the stones reminded the Hebrews that the waters of Jordan were dried up for the people to go into the promised land. The instruction of the young centered on the history, laws, and praise of God. Hebrew fathers transmitted these ideas faithfully to their children, giving them a love for freedom under God and a love for the land that God had given them. The Hebrew culture was an attachment to the land, not as an abstract idea but as a tangible reality of life-giving soil, which the Israelites could scoop up and hold in their hands.

This love for the land was true in the home schools in Athens, where fathers either taught their sons well or the son would have no obligation to support his father in old age. Even militaristic Sparta had the boys stay with their families until they were seven years old. Girls were taught by their mothers to be keepers of the house and to be good mothers of Spartan warriors. After the Spartan soldier retired from military service at the age of thirty, the citizen was required to marry and was given land to work for the support of his family. Under the Roman republic, the fathers, whose wealth was measured by the land they owned, prided themselves in being able to instruct their own sons. Only under the empire were boys subjected to the brutality of the public grammar schools, with monotonous recitations and constant beatings.

Later, in the colonies and in England, fathers and mothers instructed their children in the home. Almost all of the colonists were people of the soil, taking from the earth the abundance, and using the land to live. The yeoman farmers were free men, self-sufficient in the keenest sense. Sons and daughters were taught to love the land, to enjoy the liberty that only ownership of productive land can give, and to work with nature, not against it. The small farmers in the North, South, and West developed a culture, a life that was deep in the soil of the land, which gave stability and permanence. Industrialized societies are incapable of providing permanence.

4. Foundations: The Home School and Culture

Industrialism is man-made, but the earth is the Lord's. Factories decay, but the land ever lives.

Thus, if not in a literal sense then at least in a figurative one, every home school—past and present—is an attempt to return to the soil, to dig into the earth, to establish a monument as a testimony that this plot of land is what the Lord has given to possess. And for this reason, as the peaceful, unhurried life of the yeoman farmer is thought to be an oddity in a land of machinery, skyscrapers, and computer terminals, the home school seems an aberration among the programmed, industrialized schools of modern America. In their hearts and minds, home educators are motivated—consciously or unconsciously—to preserve a culture, something with permanence in a transitory world.

In the September 3, 1782, issue of the *Parker's General Advertiser and Morning Intelligencer*, John Adams stated, "But manufactures are not the foundations of [America's] commerce, nor is commerce her great means of acquiring wealth. Agriculture, and the continued augmentation of the value of land by improvement, are the great source of her wealth." The hearts of young students are likened unto fertile ground; however, like the Romans spreading salt upon the soil of Carthage, industrialism spoils these hearts with the love of money. On the other hand, because it has sympathy with the values of agrarianism, only the home school resting on culturalism possesses the proper values and beliefs worthy enough to be presented to the next generation.

MANNERS
The Fine Art of Living

The adoption of vice has, I am convinced, ruined ten times more young men than natural inclinations.

—PHILIP DORMER STANHOPE,
Fourth Earl of Chesterfield *Letters . . . to His Son*

Who is a wise man and endued with knowledge among you? let him shew out of a good conversation his works with meekness of wisdom.

—JAMES 3:13

Even the reconstructionist cannot create new institutions from nothing. Current materials must be used to fashion the improved would-be society. But the dilemma for reconstructionists is that since they cannot create anything with new materials, they must then raze the institutions for materials found in the current society. Therefore, reconstructionists do not build anything, but rather they destroy everything worthwhile, including manners and grace. The student as machine is told what to do; however, the student as a soul is shown what to do. Since imitation is the essence of pure education, the student will need good examples to emulate. Should the student not be introduced to the best and noblest patterns found in the world of letters and art, educators will dishonor their culture and will maim their students.

Indeed, without good examples, the student will adopt poor ones among the miscreants of humanity. For this reason, Chesterfield admonishes his son to avoid taking up the bad habits of other men, because the boy will have enough personal faults with which to contend. According to Chesterfield, life is a fine art that must be developed well and that can be fully appreciated only by the pure. Agreeing with this is Emerson, who states in his speech "Progress of Culture" that the "foundation of culture, as of character, is at last the moral sentiment." While the end of pure education is the student's love of God and neighbor, a by-product on the way toward these goals is necessarily the cultivation of the student and the refinement of tastes. Therefore, moral sentiment manifests itself by the display of cultivated manners, which marks ladies and gentlemen and sets them apart as the guardians of the fine art of living.

Viewing American society in the context of hypocrisy and duplicity, writers like Edith Wharton and poets like Robert Frost suggest that the modern attempt to cultivate manners, which adhere to obsolete forms, is futile. Their condemnation is just. But by condemning the genteel tradition, Wharton and Frost subconsciously reveal that cultivation is much more than external pretenses and affected politeness. Anyone can read about etiquette and practice the principles in a book. However, as a general prin-

5. Manners: The Fine Art of Living

ciple for manners, the golden rule is paramount, which insists that common courtesy springs up from within the soul.

Ideas such as kindness, generosity, and respect presuppose that other human beings are worthy of such values. Tragically, technology and progress fail to offer students the Emersonian foundation of moral sentiment. For the most part, the trained workforce consists of alienated men and women who see themselves as equals in every respect and who find it hard to discover anything to respect in themselves, much less in others. Indeed, if the soul is unlovely or lacking, then the display of feigned courtesy and decorum becomes boorish and ridiculous. Sadly, instead of the golden rule, conventional wisdom teaches us a Hobbesian first-strike rule: Stab the next fellow before he gets a chance to stab you. In this state of affairs, ladies and gentlemen simply cannot and do not exist. Competition ensures that living is a mechanical process to be fine-tuned, not a fine art to be nurtured. Since technocrats and social scientists direct the movements of a mechanical humanity, the role of ladies and gentlemen as the guardians of ideas and values is perceived as obsolete. Not surprisingly then, the modern, industrialized state, with its amoral school system, is incapable of producing any ladies and gentlemen. If young people have a semblance of manners, they learned them from their parents.

Indeed, America badly needs a revival of a gentry class among her citizens. For the most part, the modern czar in business or government makes a poor example of a lady or gentleman. Citizens pour justified contempt upon the heads of whining leaders, who fail rhetorically to win support for their ideas, whether those ideas are political, economic, or social. Truly democratic leaders will always reflect the sentiments of their underlying culture and neighborhood values. Yet modern politicians are certainly true to their technocratic leanings whenever they try to force their anti-cultural legislation upon the nation's citizens and to self-anoint themselves as priests of superior moral understanding, even though their immorality exceeds the common citizen's scruples. This moral failure on the part of current leaders reflects the milksops' incessant love for money and power, the root of all their evils. When the ultimate value in life is reduced to accumulating money and power for the sake of power, then generosity and kindness must be set aside for blatant selfishness and lying. Whenever immoral leaders control economic and political institutions, fair dealings in business and just laws from government will become impossible. An evil tree cannot produce good fruit.

In the past, American thinkers and writers have portrayed their ideal of the genteel classes. According to John Adams and Thomas Jefferson, the gentleman was an educated, privileged elitist among the planter classes. In addition to this, both men believed that the status of a gentleman was connected with birth. But history shows that the privileged birth of a scoundrel does not automatically allow him to have the right to be called a gentleman. On the other hand, the defender of the agrarian, or yeoman, gentleman was James Fenimore Cooper, whose writings include *The Deerslayer* and *The Last of the Mohicans*. Cooper's heroes all strengthen the idea of a gentleman who rises above self to display courage and integrity. The antebellum writer Nathaniel Beverley Tucker describes the Southern gentleman in his prophetic novel *The Partisan Leader*. According to Tucker, "Frank, affable, generous and kind, [the gentleman's] deportment was marked by that self-respectful courtesy which has all the good effect of dignity, without ever passing by

5. Manners: The Fine Art of Living

that name." Perhaps Tucker comes close to the mark here, because truly cultivated manners are unpretentious, just as true elegance does not draw attention to itself. The heroes and gentlemen in the novel, Douglas Trevor and his uncle, Bernard Trevor, were quiet about minding their own business and only became involved in the business of others when they were asked.

About the same time as Tucker was writing, Ralph Waldo Emerson was speaking to audiences about his transcendentalism. During his many talks, Emerson attempted to formulate the eclectic gentleman, the true democrat. Describing the so-called privileged class, with its love for money, Emerson was quite certain that no perfect gentleman could be found within its ranks. In his essay "Manners," Emerson states that gentlemen composed a "fraternity of the best." If what Emerson says is true, then by producing only an army of average workers, governmental education will supply few prospective candidates for the fraternity of the best—if any at all. But to even suggest that there exists a "best" requires a set of values and standards by which the gentleman can be measured. These standards are not difficult to apply if the society has heroes. Unfortunately, Americans have abused the word *hero* by claiming that anyone who shows up for work is a hero. Nevertheless, when a society can no longer believe in heroes, determining what is meant by the best becomes very difficult.

Ours is a society in need of real heroes, gallant souls who show bravery and have nobility of purpose. To be sure, according to Thomas Carlyle, the marks of a dying society are the inability to believe in heroes and a bias to debunk its national heroes of the past. Perhaps the reason why natives of the South still have a semblance of regional pride and a culture is that their past heroes—Jefferson Davis, Alexander Stephens, John C. Calhoun, Robert E. Lee, Stonewall Jackson, and dozens of others—retain a dignified place of honor in the minds and hearts of most Southerners.

On the other hand, when one contrasts this respect for Southern heroes to the denigration of national heroes like Thomas Jefferson and George Washington in the mass media and public schools, one cannot but wonder whether madness has become the norm. Many public schools have changed their names by removing *George Washington*, because the first president of the United States had at one time owned slaves. This insanity results from social engineers judging the past by a current standard, which is purely arbitrary nonsense. However, instead of being saddened, Washington undoubtedly would be relieved to know that his name is no longer being associated with the travesty of public education, because he would have had better sense than to be mixed up with it in the first place. Yet while American society is decaying for want of worthy heroes, modern youth have embraced varlets of the worst sort.

Who are the heroes of the American youth? Like any vacuum, if one eliminates past heroes, the void must be replaced with someone or something else. Men worship other men in the sense that some men are deemed worthy to receive praise and honor. At the heart of hero-worship is the desire to imitate the hero. Some kind of hero will be followed and emulated as an example, either by recognized genuine worthiness or by apathetic default.

Once again, Emerson reminds us that moral sentiment is the root of good manners and of being a gentleman, and moral sentiment is composed of values. However, since values can be either good or bad, positive or negative, the educator must ensure that the student has the best heroes to emulate, for the kinds of values espoused by our heroes are important. It seems that reading literature, which includes the belles lettres and history, provides the best source for worthy heroes. Several studies have been conducted since the year 1900 regarding heroes in the lives of American youths. The table below reflects how young people's heroes have changed over a fifty-year period.

	1900	1950
Historical figures	78%	33%
Literary figures	12%	0%
Relatives	10%	10%
Sports, musicians, and movie stars	0%	57%

Even though only two percent of American households had a television set in 1949, these figures reflect the impact that radio, movies, and spectator sports had on forming the youths' adoption of heroes. In spring 2000, a follow-up study asked the following open-ended question: "Who do you admire the most, who do you look up to, and who would you trade places with?" The overwhelming choice of today's youth was, first, television and movie stars; second, rock musicians; and third, professional athletes. Today, no one should be surprised to learn nothing has changed. A little reflection will reveal that each group of individuals has much in common. Clearly, all are rich and famous entertainers. But the reason for this is all are creatures of the media, which hard sells the public to buy unnecessary products that center on entertainment. In addition to this, these individuals are selling something to the public, whether the items are movie tickets or athletic shoes. These "heroes" do not engender noble character but prey on emotions by endorsing—for a fee—charities asking for financial support for hungry children, the vulnerable elderly, and the seriously ill. Yet if every movie star, rock musician, and athlete were to disappear from the earth today, American society would do quite well without these spokespersons. Therefore, these heroes, falsely so called, do not enrich an individual's life; rather, the rogues enrich themselves by taking from the consumer without giving anything of lasting value in return. These charlatans, then, are not heroes at all.

Like the Greeks, who made gods in their own image, the tendency of the uncultivated soul is to always adopt the worst traits and habits of other people. The soul who would be a lady or a gentleman must have heroes worthy of emulation who will help lift the gentle soul above the mediocrity of the current age. To whom should budding ladies and gentlemen look to as heroes? For all children, the search should go no further than looking to their mother and father. But more than likely, modern youngsters have a contempt for their parents, who both may work in menial jobs just to make ends meet. No culture is developed in the household, no traditions are deemed worthy to be passed down, and no sense of purpose exists other than finding sufficient entertainment between paychecks. The only influence that the parents may offer to their children will be a negative example of what the youth does not want to become: static, in a rut, and always broke. Therefore, to the American teenager, simply having lots of money is seen as the way out of boredom and into a world of nice cars, big houses, and beautiful people. In other words, today's students visualize a world of endless entertainment where they are the star performers, but the appearance is a world of make-believe, which often ends in the reality of suicide, which is hero-worship of the self.

5. Manners: The Fine Art of Living

In his book *A Confession*, Leo Tolstoy remarks that suicide reflects the ultimate act of bravery, since the individual committing suicide finally faces the reality that life is a sham and has no meaningful purpose. According to Tolstoy, life is not just gloomy and disheartening but it also ends in total failure, which is death itself. So why not end life now and avoid the sickness and misery, since death is inevitable? The brave will. However, Tolstoy states that the vast majority of people are cowards. Since they lack the fortitude to kill themselves, people merely resign themselves to a miserable existence, getting along in their lives the best they can.

But what Tolstoy mistakes as cowardice is actually self-control. Studies show that most suicides involve a dulling of the inhibitions with alcohol or other drugs. Perhaps distressed souls keep living because they have the confident belief that they will find happiness someday, and they would hate to miss their happiness whenever it arrives. In Tolstoy's case, God found him and became his happiness and joy. What Tolstoy fails to give credit to is his self-discipline, the suppressing of his natural inclinations of ending it all. One of the hardest lessons for ladies and gentlemen is the mastery of themselves. Teachers and parents can help their students toward discipline, but in the end, self-discipline is accomplished by the students.

Under self-discipline, three major skills needing perfecting relate to the appetites, the passions, and the tongue. Whether drinking or eating, the appetites ought to be done in moderation. A lady or gentleman is not a glutton. Yet America is the land of gluttony, where she sanctions drunkenness and overeating. Being overweight can be a physical ailment; however, in most cases, Americans' obsession with pudginess is the symptom of laziness, of bad food choices, and of no self-control. The overweight professor behind the desk or the corpulent sheriff running for reelection is just as contemptible as the drunkard passed out on a sidewalk.

Not only do gentlepersons control their appetites, but they check their passions as well. Nothing displays greater boorishness than unrestrained fits of anger or callow complaining. The gentleman ought to hold his temper, because his arguments should be based on supportable facts, not on emotional appeals. Weak minds offering even weaker rhetoric always resort to name-calling and appalling diatribes. Let it never be said of a gentleman that he lost his cool or that he allowed his opponent to see him sweat under pressure.

But the most important skill of all to be learned by ladies and gentlemen is the mastery of their tongues. Indeed, perhaps the student would do well to learn to keep silent most of the time. The greatest peacemaker of all is the one who can control everyone else, not by presenting compelling reasons and support, but by saying nothing at all. But when the mouth is opened to speak, the gentleperson should offer words seasoned with grace and wisdom. The Bible offers many fine examples when harsh words and rude speech engendered strife and hatred. While being men and women of conviction, gentlepersons hasten not to create conflicts but rather to solve them. After all, self-discipline promotes the doing of what is right and the eschewing of what is wrong.

Aristotle believed that the happy person is the moral one. Indeed, life cannot have much pleasure for evildoers if they are constantly looking over their shoulders ensuring that no one is sneaking up behind them to get even. However, humankind has had sufficient time to prove that moral perfection cannot be achieved

5. Manners: The Fine Art of Living

through willpower or good habits alone. Ladies and gentlemen need additional strength, because self-control and good manners require careful attention and cultivation. The superiority of the home school becomes therefore apparent, because gentlepersons are the result of *homes*. While moral instruction is absolutely necessary for the student, living by example is best. Since only homes have a differentiation between the genders, the parents ought to be the heroes of their children.

A man and a woman can both be police officers, and both genders have demonstrated competence in their duties. However, women can only become doctors, lawyers, soldiers, and truck drivers by sacrificing their modesty. In his *Republic*, Plato insists that the perfect state must do away with the notion of the home, with its values relating to personal relationships. So long as women insist on maintaining their modesty, the state cannot control the children of its citizens. Therefore, women, and particularly mothers, become the key in the preservation of any society.

If the parents were the heroes in the home, the sons would want to be like their fathers, and daughters would desire to be like their mothers. Therefore, the parents need to constantly cultivate their own manners and tastes, while fathers guard their integrity and while mothers maintain their modesty. This, of course, means saturating the home with the best in books, music, and art. The best literature will have the best heroes. In fact, the one book that is most instructive regarding the making of a gentleman is not a book about etiquette, but Daniel Defoe's *Robinson Crusoe*.

Crusoe rises above his circumstances, which looked very bleak indeed. On his island, the castaway creates a culture of self-sufficiency, industry, and thrift. His own soul was nourished with periods of devotion and contemplation, which produced a man who was courageous in battle, resourceful in want, and gracious in conduct with friends, enemies, and servants. This is not to say that Crusoe was without faults. Sometimes his fears and emotions got the better of his reason and faith, but these were aberrations of his character, not the substance of it. While he was at first alienated from the whole world, Crusoe was not alienated from himself nor from God. But when society came calling to his island, Crusoe became the gentleman.

If self-sufficiency, moral courage, and self-government—as opposed to governmental doles, contemptible whining, and technocracy—are to survive as American ideals, then the home school becomes all important in the creation of a new genteel class. Home school students under pure education will as a matter of course become more refined in their manners and tastes. The new class of ladies and gentlemen will be those with a bent toward self-discipline, a desire for learning, and a love for neighbors. From this class will arise the future leaders of the nation. The gentlemen ought to become leaders in the government and in the colleges and universities.

All home-schooled gentlemen should consider getting a liberal arts degree with studies in literature, history, and philosophy. A gentleman will not waste his time or money on a business degree or other vocational training like engineering and medicine. Occupational fields do not need gentlemen, because these endeavors require technicians, whose constant repetition of a task is their only claim to proficiency. If a student balks at the idea that a liberal arts education does not pay as well as a doctor, then the love of money is driving the student, not his love for his neighbor. The need today

5. Manners: The Fine Art of Living

is not more scientists, engineers, or physicians. The home school gentlemen should have better and loftier goals in life than learning a process that generates a steady flow of income from consumers.

After securing a college degree, the gentleman should consider attending law school, but not necessarily for the purpose of practicing law. The United States does not need more lawyers. Contrary to popular belief, law schools do not teach law. Rather, thinking is taught, ideas are scrutinized, and values are tested. With a law degree, the gentleman has several possible directions to travel, but hopefully he will consider the road to becoming a statesman, whether in local, state, or national levels of leadership. Nevertheless, whether he goes to law school or not, the gentleman must get advanced degrees. The advanced degree helps the gentleman to become an expert in a particular area of study, and it is necessary to teach at the college level as well. The influence that a professor has over a class of college students is enormous. Professors of literature, history, and philosophy have created great changes in society, for good and for ill. Professors not only teach, but they do research and write papers and books as well. The home school could very easily restore the distinguished statesman and scholar to America by replacing the current cheap politician and post-modern existentialist.

The reader will note that the mention of the Gospel ministry is conspicuously absent from the above discussion. The callings of statesmanship and professorship are natural callings of the gentleman. However, the calling of the preacher is from God, which takes precedence over all other callings. The Bible is clear that pastors must show hospitality, moderation, and peacefulness with fellow Christians. But the alien idea of the preacher being a slick salesman offering psychological quips in order to entertain the masses is a strange American phenomenon not warranted by the Bible. When one considers the preachers found in the Bible, like Elijah, Jeremiah, John the Baptist, Paul, and even the Lord Jesus Christ, one seldom sees kindness, gentleness, and tolerance expressed in the society in which they lived. These preachers certainly were not avoiding hurting anyone's thin-skinned sensibilities. The purpose of the preacher is not to make friends, to be a nice guy, or even to preserve a culture, but to root up and destroy sin. The preacher is to drive men to the light or further into darkness, for he offers a message that is either life unto life or death unto death. There is very little preaching in the United States today. This is true, because most modern preachers placate wickedness and lack a final authority that is trustworthy.

Even more urgent than having gentlemen and preachers is the need for America to have ladies. The lady should have the qualities of kindness, intelligence, and respect for others, or in other words, she will closely adhere to the golden rule. However, the distinguishing mark of a true lady is that she will be modest and will avoid notoriety. The moment a young woman desires to be the life of the party, she is no longer, according to Tucker, "fit to be the wife of a Virginia gentleman." The point here is that good manners will not attract attention to the lady herself.

Therefore, a lady is marked by her behavior. Indeed, the central test of a young lady is her domestic behavior at home. If she is considerate to her siblings and obedient to her parents, then she is a lady of the finest sort. Also important is her behavior in public, which relates to her modesty. Ladies should not seek positions in business, politics, and other spheres of notoriety. This statement will seem appallingly chauvinistic to shallow thinkers or to those who have accepted uncritically the feminist theory. Few today would be foolish enough to defend the unreasonable position that men can do a better job than women in management and the workforce as problem solvers. Women across the world have shown they are very capable of being adept to business, politics, and the arts.

On the other hand, most working mothers will reluctantly admit that if they had a choice to stay home with their children or to work outside the home, the overwhelming response would be to stay home. What makes women so valuable to any society is not their abilities to master processes or even to grapple with the problems of business, law, and politics. The reason that women are the most valuable citizens in society is because all women excel at developing human relationships. Therefore, the greatest influence that a true lady can have in this lifetime is within the confines and in the context of her home. Indeed, the lady makes the home, and she nurtures the next generation of ladies and gentlemen through the home school. While not for the purpose of a career, home-schooled ladies should go to college to get a degree in education, preferably in elementary education, with a minor in one of the humanities. When the young lady gets married, the degree will be helpful with her own home school. But also, if anything ever happens to her husband, the lady at least has the wherewithal to span the emergency. But her goal, indeed her consuming desire, ought to be to make a home a place of learning and security.

Therefore, the gentleman should seek roles in the government and higher education, and the lady should seek making a home and a school. To predict how much longer the present United States will continue to exist is difficult. The simple act of voting seems to be called into question, as well as whether a constitution that was created under the ideas of an agrarian republic is workable under a technocratic empire. May an army of ladies and gentlemen come quickly in order to provide sanity to a people who are beginning to lose all hope in a future.

06 WORK AND LEISURE
The Forgotten Arts

So here upon my back I'll lie
And look my fill into the sky.

—EDNA ST. VINCENT MILLAY, *"Renascence"*

And he said unto them, Come ye yourselves apart into a desert place, and rest a while: for there were many coming and going, and they had no leisure so much as to eat.

—MARK 6:31

Most Americans would think that those who lie on their backs, staring straight up into the sky, must surely be idlers of the worst sort. For what purpose does looking up into the sky provide to the gazer of nothingness? For the poetess of "Renascence," this gazing merely caused the rebirth of her soul. The above question could be asked of David when he wonders, "When I consider thy heavens, the work of thy fingers, the moon and the stars, which thou hast ordained; What is man, that thou art mindful of him? and the son of man, that thou visitest him?" (Psalm 8:3–4). Such questions require sitting still and thinking. However, the industrialized American has "better things to do" and is always wanting to do something. What this something is, no one knows for sure. But this much is certain: admiring a star-studded sky or perusing a book in an ancient tongue is considered a waste of time. Yet the modern go-getter fails to reflect for a moment that staring at a television set at home, a glass of beer on a bar, or a sporting event in a stadium not only is truly a waste of time but also marks a life without purpose. Indeed, Americans excel at ensuring that their lives are squandered with meaningless activity, whether at work or play, and when life is over, they can boast of few accomplishments but harbor many regrets.

This animosity toward "loafing" suggests that industrialism either has destroyed leisure in America or at least has misdirected it. How ironic! The priests of industry promised the brotherhood of human resources that labor-saving contraptions would increase leisure, and eventually, even the laborer would become part of the leisure class. Perhaps workers have done so, in the sense that they exert very little energy on most jobs. However, even though Americans seem to have more free time, the prophesy has proven to be a lie. By a sleight of hand, like the announcing of the drop in crime only because the government legalized improper behavior or ignored it, industrialism has redefined leisure, because the nature of work has radically changed. But instead of stoning the false prophets, Americans become more wild, trying desperately to find some meaning—indeed, any purpose—for life.

This desperate search for meaning results from the United States being filled with unhappy people. The theme parks, the

6. Work and Leisure: The Forgotten Arts

sporting events, and the rock concerts do not reveal the laughter of joy, because if people were to listen closely, they will hear the cries of despair and anguish coming from a sick society. Americans are not having a good time when they have to pay enormous sums of money to escape from their daily monotony. Pushing keys and flipping hamburgers, whether grilled or fried, fail to give an employee a sense of personal accomplishment. This work is dehumanizing, and industrialized citizens reveal the degradation of their souls by drinking booze to forget momentarily, by watching a boxing match to see blood, and by switching channels to find anything of interest for non-thinkers. Since Americans refuse to sit for one moment to reflect, it never occurs to them that perhaps the one thing needful in their lives is just to sit still and reflect.

Since the days of Adam, human activity has been divided into three segments, which are nearly equal in length: work, leisure, and sleep. In the modern industrial society, work has been defined as that portion of life when the time is spent for acquiring things. For the farmer, this means tilling the soil and harvesting the crops. For the worker in factories or offices, this means selling one's time for a paycheck. Leisure connotes free time that belongs to individuals to do whatever they wish to do during breaks, lunch, and after work. Of course, sleep is enjoyed by most people, unless one has installment payments that are overdue with no money in the bank. Then sleep seems to steal away even from the most tired of souls.

Most Americans dislike their jobs, and if they do like what they are doing, they never feel that the compensation is sufficient for their time. Their free time is frittered away by going to night clubs, by going to circuses to see savage sports, like hockey and football, and by watching ridiculous programs on television. Why should anybody wonder that Americans feel that they lack purpose and accomplishments in life? All of these activities reflect the bankruptcy of the human soul that refuses to think deeply about life, because to do so will cause the thinker to feel too much pain. A can of beer is the choice for those who hate to think at all.

However, the modern definition for *work* and *leisure* evolves from the context of this technological age, which has corrupted so many values. While work, leisure, and sleep should constitute the time of every human being, the popular meaning of these activities has unfortunately led to confusion and frustration among Americans. In reality, most work has become leisure, where minds, not muscle, are used, and leisure has become entertainment, where time is wasted, rather than used for intellectual and moral betterment of the individual. No wonder Americans are in pitiful shape both physically and mentally. Implied in the modern meanings of *work* and *leisure* are the ideas of bondage and freedom. However, while an employee must certainly do the bidding of his master who pays his salary, the activity during this time may not be work at all. Likewise, the activity during free time may not be leisure. For an example, while he is on the job, a police officer is not "working" if he is cruising in his patrol car. The officer is thinking, observing, and listening, which are activities that require no physical *work*. On the other hand, the officer is working whenever he walks into a doughnut shop for a cup of coffee or chases a suspect on foot. These activities require bodily movement and are properly called *work*. At least this is what Lamech understood work to mean when he named Noah, who was a "comfort" in spite of the work and toil of his father's hands to make the land productive (Genesis 5:29). According to Webster's Dictionary of 1828, this is how Ameri-

6. Work and Leisure: The Forgotten Arts

cans used to understand *work:* "1. Labor; employment; exertion of strength; particularly in man, manual labor." Only industrialism tries to divide work into physical and mental labor. Yet no one has ever broken into a sweat reading a book or even writing one.

The truth of the matter is that *all* time is free time, which the individual freely determines how every minute will be used, guided by no universal law decreeing otherwise. This includes sleep as well. Some blessed folks need only two hours of sleep a day, as it was reported of Henry II of England. Perhaps the reason for the astonishing number of inventions by Thomas Edison was the inventor's little need for sleep. Whenever he became tired, Edison would sit in a chair, would hold a spoon between two fingers, and would then close his eyes. As soon as the spoon fell to the floor, the sound would awaken Edison, who was now refreshed to continue his experiments. Yet for most Americans, if it were not for the obligation to earn a paycheck to pay their debts, the nation's human resources would be contented to spend much more time sleeping than would be necessary.

Not only is the dichotomy of "on-the-job vs. free time" meaningless because all time is free, but the idea of a laboring class and a leisure class also fails to define *work* and *leisure*. This dichotomy remains a popular notion and is closely related to education. In his book *Up from Slavery*, Booker T. Washington states that the ex-slaves believed that getting an education meant not having to labor: "The idea, however, was too prevalent that, as soon as one secured a little education, in some unexplainable way he would be free from most of the hardships of the world, and, at any rate, could live without manual labor."

Of course, the ex-slaves believed this because they observed the lives of their masters, who were educated and who were "gentlemen of leisure." Since the escape from menial labor is considered a worthy goal, teachers and parents have convinced young people that a college education is the ticket to a good job, which implies little or no labor for big bucks. But the so-called leisure class based on education is a myth when one considers that auto mechanics command top dollar, while some PhDs end up becoming drivers of "eighteen-wheelers." While truck driving is an honorable profession, potential drivers need just a little training to become successful in their field. Even though drivers make better than average money, the life on the road is not any easy one, and most individuals are unwilling to forego a social life. The myth of "more education, more money" is nonsense.

Perhaps to rediscover the proper meaning of *work* and *leisure*, we must appeal to the poets and men of letters, who can sense the difference between these two activities better than the rest of us mortals. In England during the late eighteenth century, large landowners restricted the use of lands that before were held in common and used particularly for the farmers' livestock. The restricted land was now reserved for the landowners' exclusive use, which typically meant the land became unproductive or used for sport. By the thousands, small-scale farmers left their farms and went to the cities, looking for jobs in the factories. The overcrowded cities became slums, which soon fostered crime and spread disease. For industrialized England, the farmer was no longer necessary, because raw materials and food could be imported from the Empire's colonies.

In "The Deserted Village," Oliver Goldsmith depicts the demise of a small country village due to the Enclosure Acts. In the poem,

6. Work and Leisure: The Forgotten Arts

Goldsmith attacks the concentration of resources in the hands of the wealthy and the removal of the yeoman farmers and small shopkeepers to the big cities. This lengthy poem of 430 lines has a clear theme:

> *Ill fares the land, to hastening ills a prey,*
> *Where wealth accumulates, and men decay;*
> *Princes and lords may flourish, or may fade;*
> *A breath can make them, as a breath has made:*
> *But a bold peasantry, their country's pride,*
> *When once destroyed, can never be supplied.*

Goldsmith points out that when moneygrubbing becomes a greater value than the preservation of the small farmer, then this is a sure symptom of a very sick society. The "nobility" is always self-perpetuating by fiat, but the destruction of the farmer is permanent. Seldom, if ever, do office or factory workers decide to quit their jobs to become gentleman farmers. In addition to this, the labor of the farmer—as well as the coal miner, the steel worker, or the tire mechanic—is honorable and bold work. Thus, work is connected with physical strength. Indeed, Thomas Carlyle states, "It has been written, 'An endless significance lies in Work'; a man perfects himself by working." To Carlyle, all true work is noble, whether that work is done by a yeoman farmer or by a factory hand.

Goldsmith and Carlyle were at *leisure* to glorify labor, because they were in the position to write, "Know thy work and do it." While both of these men were part of the true leisure class, they were not part of the wealthy aristocracy. Often, the aristocrat possessed no true wealth. To illustrate this false nobility, Charles Dickens uses a common boy who wants to be a gentleman for all of the wrong reasons. In *Great Expectations*, Pip believes that being a gentleman with financial means qualifies him for a life of leisure, luxury, and liberty to woo Estella, a lady. But only after he loses almost everything that is worthwhile, including his self-respect, does Pip discover that he was deceived by his observations and passions. The true man of leisure is not marked by outward trappings of worldly success but rather by the inward possession of intellectual and spiritual wealth that can neither be inherited nor bought at any price.

Therefore, wealthy men are not automatically part of the so-called leisure class, although being independently wealthy certainly does help. If he has to eke out a living, a farmer may not have the opportunity to achieve greatness, as expressed in Thomas Gray's "Elegy Written in a Country Churchyard":

> *Perhaps in this neglected spot is laid*
> *Some heart once pregnant with celestial fire;*
> *Hands, that the rod of empire might have sway'd,*
> *Or waked to ecstasy the living lyre:*
> *But Knowledge to their eyes her ample page,*
> *Rich with the spoils of time, did ne'er unroll;*
> *Chill Penury repress'd their noble rage,*
> *And froze the genial current of the soul.*

Gray wonders that perhaps in these forgotten graves of hard-working commoners there could have been the remains of an "inglorious Milton" or a "Cromwell, guiltless of his country's blood." The reason why the commoners could not reach their creative and

6. Work and Leisure: The Forgotten Arts

political genius was due to the necessity to labor, to work the land in order to live. Had they been fortunate to experience the accident of birth into a wealthy family, then they, too, could have had the opportunity to achieve fame in letters and politics, which were the privileges of the men of wealth and aristocracy. However, Gray's complaint, as well as Goldsmith's, is that most of the wealthy did not take advantage of their privilege. While the yeoman farmer quietly plowed his fields, the wealthy, for the most part, wasted their time with frivolity and entertainment. In short, the aristocrats failed to be examples of what is both pure and noble.

Thus, Gray provides a key to the nature of work and leisure. The activity of work requires use of the human body, and leisure centers on the creation of literature, poetry, and the arts, the contemplation of life and death, or the leading of a nation. In other words, *work* relates to physical exertion, whereas *leisure* relates to metaphysical activities, while *sleep* rejuvenates both the physical and metaphysical elements of human beings.

Not only Thomas Gray but also Henry David Thoreau understood the meanings of work and leisure. In his book *Walden*, Thoreau relates his two-year experiment when he lived in a simple cabin beside Walden Pond, which was about a mile from Concord, Massachusetts. Thoreau notes that work is required for supplying four essentials for human survival: food, shelter, clothing, and fuel. All of these items require some amount of physical labor. If one is self-sufficient, then bodily exercise is required to grow a garden, build shelter, make clothing, and provide firewood. As soon as they adequately provide for these necessities of life, individuals can then enjoy intellectual pursuits, or leisure. Yet Thoreau laments,

But men labor under a mistake. The better part of the man is soon ploughed into the soil for compost. By a seeming fate, commonly called necessity, they are employed, as it says in an old book, laying up treasures which moth and rust will corrupt and thieves break through and steal. It is a fool's life, as they will find when they get to the end of it, if not before.

Thoreau expresses a firm dislike for those who plant more than they need, because overproduction requires more manual labor and time, which could be more profitably used for developing the intellect. However, after he provides for his own necessities, even Thoreau plants a field of beans, an amount which he claims to have been seven miles in length, if the rows were joined end to end. Thoreau remarks that he is not sure why he planted beans in particular. In fact, according to Thoreau, selling the crop was the most difficult part of all! However, he loved his work.

What shall I learn of beans or beans of me? I cherish them, I hoe them, early and late I have an eye to them; and this is my day's work. It is a fine broad leaf to look on. My auxiliaries are the dews and rains which water this dry soil, and what fertility is in the soil itself, which for the most part is lean and effete.

Echoing Carlyle's thoughts, Thoreau sees nobility in purposeful labor. Of course, Thoreau's purpose was to work with and to understand nature, which is not a bad purpose at all. The work of planting, hoeing, and harvesting was physical and tiring. To be sure, this effort produced dignified sweat. After the chores in the field were over, Thoreau would often take a romp in the woods for more exercise of the body. But even more important, his moments of leisure were well used. Modern Americans would consider Thoreau to be a consummate loafer. Perhaps he was—but he loafed well. On

6. Work and Leisure: The Forgotten Arts

a small table rested a copy of Homer's *Iliad* in classical Greek. His leisure was occupied with reading the classics and sitting under trees, standing beside brooks, and studying nature and people. Thoreau knew the poverty of most souls for want of seeking intellectual leisure:

A man, any man, will go considerably out of his way to pick up a silver dollar; but here are golden words [the ancient classics], *which the wisest men of antiquity have uttered, and whose worth the wise of every succeeding age have assured us of;—and yet we learn to read only as far as Easy Reading, the primers and classbooks, and when we leave school, the "Little Reading," and story books, which are for boys and beginners; and our reading, our conversation and thinking, are all on a very low level, worthy only of pygmies and manikins.*

If this was true in the early nineteenth century, then how much lower have "our reading, our conversation and thinking" fallen? Today, most jobs require little, if any, physical labor—or thinking. Instead of suffering from sore arms and backs, Americans spend millions of dollars preventing or correcting carpal tunnel syndrome and obesity. On the other hand, one is more likely to get seriously injured doing any number of so-called leisure activities, such as participating in sports and gardening. Oddly, these activities require more energy than the monotonous pushing of buttons on the job. Perhaps the shifting of leisure during work and work during leisure would not be so bad if Americans were getting enough work and leisure. But unfortunately, after "a hard day's work in the office," staring at a computer monitor for eight hours, the worker is too tired to do anything except to stare at a television set in the evening. Therefore, neither the mind nor the body is ever employed. Laziness represents the modern definition of leisure, which is a far cry from philosophical reflection.

Since the metaphysical belongs in the domain of leisure, Americans have done a great disservice to the nation's youth by having them believe that studying and going to school is work, when it is nothing of the kind. Even ministers of the Gospel are without clean hands. When exhorting the flock to know the will of God, preachers insist that the student's vocation is to study hard, because God has given the young person the job of being a student at this time in life.

However, the mass exodus of children from the homes nearly every morning in America is not the will of God but the will of the government. The Lord would never participate in such a sad enterprise. While held captive in their classrooms, the students are admonished to do their "school work," which includes both "seat work" and "homework." But how can this be *work* when no physical effort is expended? On the other hand, recess from this "work" is eagerly awaited by the overworked scholars, who make a mad dash to see who will get to the swings first—unless they did not work hard enough at being studious or at being good and have to be punished by sitting at their desk and by doing nothing. After becoming hot, tired, and sweaty, the happy scholars are now unable to concentrate on their work, because they are beat. Even teachers complain about being overworked. How can anyone be tired after shuffling a few papers and grading them with an answer key? What teachers should be complaining about is not work, or even leisure, but boredom. A clearer case for the ethics of "fair is foul" cannot be argued than by this activity taking place in schools across the United States.

Since Americans think that the value of learning is measured by the amount of money someone will eventually command with a "good education," then this linking of school with work should

6. Work and Leisure: The Forgotten Arts

be expected. After all, as a valuable human resource of the future, the mass-produced students are simply learning the jargon of the workplace before they take their place in American society and in the global economy.

Clearly the home school should dispel these modern notions about work and leisure. For the most part, the activities of the school should exist in the realm of leisure. The home educator should emphasize to her students that leisure used to be, and still is, reserved for the privileged of every society. Students should be grateful that they do not have to work in a bottling factory like Charles Dickens, while his family remained in debtors' prison. Furthermore, homeschool students should realize that they belong to a privileged class, which does not have to "work" in a governmental classroom, reciting rote and memorizing trivia.

In addition to learning to appreciate their leisure time to gain knowledge and wisdom, homeschool students should be made to realize that being individually tutored is a privilege that has been reserved always for children of royalty, nobility, aristocracy, and later for the well-to-do. With this shared tradition, students in the home school are in very good company, which should cause them to stand up a little bit straighter than their friends in the public schools. Since leisure is the mark of a privileged class, the home school should concentrate on metaphysical materials, such as literature, rhetoric, and moral philosophy. This is the stuff that makes literary and political leaders. These materials will affect the heart, soul, and mind of the student. Because this is true, the student should understand that *leisure* properly means *rest* from physical labor, but this does not mean merely doing nothing.

Indeed, leisure takes place whenever the student is being creative by writing poetry or playing a guitar, or is being contemplative by reading a book or just admiring a sunset. Some mental activity must be taking place if leisure is properly employed. Thinking is the key to leisure, as it insists upon deep concentration and contemplation about life. Therefore, watching a movie or television program may or may not be leisure, depending upon the amount of critical thinking involved. The reason there is little thinking in America is because there is little leisure. Therefore, it seems the better part of valor when a teacher discovers a student appearing to be daydreaming and staring out a window, that she should allow the reverie to continue. Only the Lord knows how many ideas have been squashed whenever a teacher spoke harshly, "Stop daydreaming and get back to work." However, whenever students are cleaning their rooms, playing sports, or just walking down the street, they should realize that this activity is rightfully work, and not leisure.

What about activities that are neither work nor leisure? In these cases, the activities should be avoided. For an example, watching a movie that has no redeeming value is called *entertainment*. Entertainment is not leisure; it is a waste of precious time. Indeed, anything that is purely gratuitous should be eliminated from the student's life. In other words, if it does not help the student's heart, soul, mind, or body, the activity is unnecessary and needs to be replaced with one that will help the student achieve these goals. Unnecessary activities would include all spectator sports and watching television. In fact, the television should be removed from the home—period. Frankly, life is too short and time is too valuable to throw away on foolishness.

6. Work and Leisure: The Forgotten Arts

If your children say they have nothing to do, then they should sit still and ponder why they have nothing to do. If you believe that this criterion forbids having any fun, then you should take the time and search deeply for the reasons why you are educating your children. Pure education is only for the serious educator, who wishes to pass on a legacy and a culture. This is serious business. If learning knowledge for the sake of knowledge, tending a garden, discovering a new word, shooting a few baskets, or just sitting and listening to the sounds of the birds in the morning fails to excite the student, then life is very dull indeed and lacks significant meaning.

07 THE CURRICULUM
The Means of Pure Education

God has a right hand, but is quite bereft
Of that, which we do nominate the left.

—ROBERT HERRICK, *"The Right Hand"*

Turn you to the strong hold, ye prisoners of hope: even to day do I declare that I will render double unto thee; When I have bent Judah for me, filled the bow with Ephraim, and raised up thy sons, O Zion, against thy sons, O Greece, and made thee as the sword of a mighty man.

—ZECHARIAH 9:12-13

The perfect curriculum is a myth. Because of the public schools with their emphasis on the average pupil, this myth is promulgated with a core curriculum that includes units in English, math, science, foreign languages, and history. Such approaches to learning are based on the principles of mass production and nothing else. Except for some elective courses, the individual propensities of the student are not considered at all. Unfortunately, while the home school may enjoy some flexibility regarding the particular subjects for students, the state boards of education often impose on home educators certain subjects that must be taught. Sometimes the requirement for a foreign language does not permit ancient languages like Greek and Latin but must be a modern language. Thus, it reveals the educationalists' prejudice toward utilitarian thinking, which requires all subjects to have some "practical" purpose. The evil inherent with the modern compartmentalized curriculum is that the various core subjects seem to have no relationship with one another. Teachers present history, math, science, and even literature as separate units that are very scientific in approach, with lists of facts to be memorized. The memorization of facts fails to recognize a student's uniqueness. However, if each student is unique, then the curriculum should be different for every student.

The goal of pure education is for students to love God with all of their heart, soul, mind, and strength. The evidence that students love God is by observing how they treat their neighbors. All of this is easily discovered from the Scriptures. However, the task of finding the best way to achieve this love of God and neighbor becomes a bit more complex. Since technical training can safely ignore ethics, the attempt to keep religion out of the public schools seems somewhat justifiable. For a student to identify a verb, to know that Egypt is in Africa, and to remember that $a = a$ requires no moral struggle with good and evil. But the home school does not exist to pass on processes and rote; the school is to pass on the best of a culture to its students, who will in turn enrich their culture with explicit ideas and values.

7. The Curriculum: The Means of Pure Education

Thus, the curriculum will be very different than that used in the public schools, because pure education is value-centered, whereas technical training is process-centered. Hence, material that offers values and ideas for the student should be preferred over material that centers on subjects that show how things work, such as mathematics and science.

However, the American home school with a biblical worldview has a conflict, since two different traditions oppose each other. One tradition is Western; the other is Eastern. The American is thoroughly immersed in Western ideas and thought. However, after salvation, the Christian experiences a different way of thinking. In that Christianity is derived from Judaism and uses a Jewish book for its guide, Christians have a strong intellectual tradition that is adopted from the Hebrews, who embrace Eastern thinking and mores. This tradition does not stop to ask about the existence of God. The belief in God is an axiom, a fact that needs no proving. For this reason, the Bible does not attempt to prove the existence of God but starts with "In the beginning God . . ." The emphasis found in Eastern thought is *obedience* and *adherence to strict principles*, that is, revealed revelation. Thus, one should only endeavor to obey divine law and not to actively work against it. To prove this statement at this point is unnecessary, because the Bible, the Koran, and other Eastern writings are replete with examples. Indeed, the very duty of Christians is to love their God and to love their neighbors. The way of peace, then, is through obeying the commandments, especially when the commandment is to believe on the Lord Jesus Christ and to imitate Him, who is the Christian's *example.*

Meditation is also important in the Hebrew tradition. Anyone who has thoughtfully studied the Book of Job realizes that the questions and issues raised in this oldest of biblical books are open-ended and cannot be answered glibly. "What is the Almighty, that we should serve him? and what profit should we have, if we pray unto him?" (Job 21:15) Such questions would be enough to keep a thousand philosophers actively speculating the depths of this one verse for their entire lifetimes. Often, the mediation centers on nature, as in Psalm 8. Nature is an ally with man, and man uses the earth to praise God. Therefore, the Hebrew tradition includes not only obedience to precepts that bring life and peace, but contemplation about these precepts as well.

On the other hand, American Christians are still partakers of the Western tradition as well. Most of the Western theories about ethics, politics, metaphysics, jurisprudence, and aesthetics come from the ancient Greeks and Romans, whose philosophies are centered on reason. When Socrates stated that the unexamined life is not worth living, or when Plato remarked that one ought to know himself, the emphasis is no longer on obeying a commandment but rather on breaking away from the conventional in order to exercise freedom of thought. Individualism, then, was important to the ancients as well as to the later humanists of the Renaissance. For this reason, God is not a given to the Western mind; rather, His existence must be proven logically through reason. If God cannot be proven logically, then like any figment of the imagination, God must simply be dismissed, and that without honors. A Hebrew would not use Anselm's ontological argument or Aquinas's teleological proofs to demonstrate that there is a God. Such thinking is foolishness to the Hebrews. Indeed, it is the fool who says there is no God.

But the ideas of individualism gave the Greeks the belief that perfection was not only desirable but very possible as well. The

7. The Curriculum: The Means of Pure Education

ancient Greeks understood the importance of individuality and expressed it in their literature and art, but it was the Renaissance that stirred men to desire immortality upon earth as well as immortality in the world to come. Since the emphasis of Western thought is upon humankind and its works, the Western tradition is *humanism*, and its subject matter is the *humanities*, which are reflected in both their ancient and Renaissance manifestations. In addition to this, the Western tradition shows an increasing hostility toward nature as well. Nature is to be subdued and conquered, because nature is supposedly actively working against man. Such a belief can be seen in any of Jack London's works, such as *White Fang*. The way that human beings will enslave nature to do their bidding is by keen judgment apart from any god. Therefore, what becomes important to the Western mind is a free and clear intellect.

In his essay "Why I Am Not a Christian," Bertrand Russell seems to understand this conflict between the East and West:

Conquer the world by intelligence and not merely by being slavishly subdued by the terror that comes from it. The whole conception of God is a conception derived from the ancient Oriental despotisms. It is a conception quite unworthy of free men.

After Russell "disproves" the existence of God by showing the weaknesses of various rational and moral arguments used by philosophers to prove God's existence, the twentieth-century's foremost secularist points out the ultimate end of Western thinking:

Science can help us to get over this craven fear in which mankind has lived for so many generations. Science can teach us, and I think our own hearts can teach us, no longer to look around for imaginary supports, no longer to invent allies in the sky, but rather to look to our own efforts here below to make this world a fit place to live in, instead of the sort of place that the churches in all these centuries have made it.

However, with this conclusion, Russell professes himself to be wise, only to show that he is a fool. Unfortunately, Russell is asking science to accomplish something that it cannot do. While the scientist can manipulate the physical world, science is not able to teach about or to generate ideas concerning truth, love, peace, and justice, which are "imaginary supports." Russell states that humankind must use its "own efforts here below," but the efforts are to be accomplished without the support of ideas.

Nevertheless, both Western and Hebrew thought seek the same end: the salvation of man. However, one tries to secure salvation through human reason, deductively and inductively, conquering the earth, and the other through obedience to divine revelation, imitating nature. The Greeks hoped that perfection could be achieved through deep contemplation, which would clear the mind of ignorance, would deny the bodily appetites, and would reveal ideal beauty. Expelling ignorance, fighting carnality, and appreciating beauty are most worthy of endeavors. However, as mentioned above, mediation and contemplation are values existing in Hebrew thought as well. Regarding ideas, the ancient Greeks do not really add anything significantly different to what the Hebrews had already revealed in their writings five hundred years before Socrates. However, what the Greeks did accomplish, or at least tried to accomplish, was the systematic organizing of knowledge, which every sixth grader knows is the definition for *science*.

While their philosophers were busy classifying and organizing their knowledge, the Greeks overlooked one consideration, which is conspicuously absent in their philosophies. On the other hand, the

7. The Curriculum: The Means of Pure Education

Hebrews did not ignore this particular consideration. In fact, much of the Bible deals with this "imaginary" human condition, which is sin. While the Greeks stumbled around because they could not rationally conceive the idea of sin, the Hebrews knew clearly that human perfection was impossible in this life and that sin tainted everything human, even good and noble works.

The existence as well as the nature of sin are revealed only in the revelation that God gave to humankind—the Bible. Yet when the Gospel of Christ came to the Greeks, not surprisingly, the Western church tried to reconcile Plato and Aristotle with the Bible through the church fathers and later through Aquinas and Berkeley. However, the Greek's project to discover true duty and the Hebrew's practice to obey revealed duty will never be reconciled. Nevertheless, if students are to learn to govern themselves well, they must have values, because human conduct is based on ideas. Today, the Western tradition of humanism has led men to existentialism, in which students define themselves by their own acts as they experience life; as Russell said, according to his materialistic nonsense, life is the "outcome of accidental collocations of atoms." Thus, mere human existence is based on chance.

Recognizing these two contrary ways of thinking, the Christian home educator should be careful to ensure that the humanities are filtered by the Bible. If pure education is to make the world intelligible for students in order for them to become an active participant in their culture, then the heart must be directed by the best moral guide. In addition to this, the student must be able to recognize where the Hebrew and Western traditions agree, and where they oppose each other. Otherwise, the student will fail to make sense of the world and will become confused mentally and alienated spiritually. This result of confusion and alienation was best expressed by Russell when he said that "on the firm foundation of unyielding despair . . . can the soul's habitation henceforth be safely built." On the other hand, the home school avoids existentialism, because its foundation is not "unyielding despair" but rather culture and home with commonality and stability.

Therefore, the weakness of the Western tradition is that it leads to transmitting only processes and to rejecting anything that is not derived from reason. Ideas such as the existence of God, salvation by the blood of Christ, and the resurrection of the dead are not concepts from reason, but from faith. Even though some Christians would insist that these ideas are rational, the truth of the matter is that these examples are written in a Book, a source that is believed through faith, not an argument that is proved. If the West has works of genius that are represented in literature and art, it is because the ideas were borrowed—consciously or unconsciously—from the Bible. The things that bring beauty into life can do so only by imitating the beauty and harmony that are found in the Scriptures and in nature.

However, since industrialism and technology refuse to be in harmony with nature, the superficial findings of science must be asserted as social fact. As an example, just because scientists observe enlarged pituitary glands in homosexuals during autopsies, this observation does not mean that this is the reason for one's sexual orientation. Perhaps the abnormal gland is not the cause but the *result* of immoral behavior. The only way to know for sure is to measure the pituitary gland before any individual indulges in the "alternative lifestyle," which of course is impossible to do. Yet even though the findings are clearly out of harmony with nature, the facts

7. The Curriculum: The Means of Pure Education

will be used to state a social truth, which is not truth at all. Since the Western tradition and science can only explain how things work, and even then not too well, ideas for harmonious living must come from the Hebrew tradition.

If students are subjected only to Western thinking and do not think deeply about life, then they will embrace evolution, natural selection, relativism, and worst of all, positivism, which is the belief that the only legitimate knowledge is that which is observed and that any knowledge about meaning and purpose is summarily rejected. The reason for this unwholesome state of affairs is that science and technology ignore metaphysics and ethics. On the other hand, pure education centers on achieving goals undergirded by their first principles, as expressed by Jesus Christ in the two greatest commandments. While Hebrew metaphysics and ethics are incapable of being proved by science, these disciplines are not subjective like the Greek philosophies are. Both of these disciplines do conform to reality. For the Christian, this reality is a Book that anyone can handle and read.

As a conclusion for this chapter, Charles Darwin can offer some insight about the certain future of technologically trained students who have learned their processes all too well. In his *Autobiography*, Darwin reminisces how he used to enjoy poetry, Shakespeare, and music, but now he finds these "higher tastes" to be sickening to him.

My mind seems to have become a kind of machine for grinding general laws out of large collections of fact, but why this should have caused the atrophy of that part of the brain alone, on which the higher tastes depend, I cannot conceive.... The loss of these tastes is a loss of happiness, and may possibly be injurious to the intellect, and more probably to the moral character, by enfeebling the emotional part of our nature.

The pursuit of science based on a materialistic worldview had bankrupted Darwin intellectually, emotionally, and morally, and the result was his loss of happiness. The difference between the Western and Hebrew traditions becomes now even more pronounced. Darwin had concentrated on knowledge that was *convergent*, which offers solutions to problems that can be readily transmitted to others. The two disciplines that are entirely convergent are mathematics and the sciences, which have answers that are either "right" or "wrong." On the other hand, knowledge that is *divergent* fails to have simple solutions. Most Americans avoid subjects that are divergent by nature. Courses such as moral philosophy, history, and literature fall outside the realm of logic and require tough thinking. The student is required to use the "imaginary supports" of love, beauty, and fairness in order to make sense of the subjects. Frankly, thinking is difficult, just like cultivating a garden is hard work. Poetry and music defies scientific classification; therefore, the unhappiness of Darwin was prompted by his failure to cultivate his heart, his soul, and his mind, which speak to the affections, the emotions, and the intellect of everyone.

When Jesus Christ reminded his listeners about the two greatest commandments, the Lord cordially invited everyone to join the human race. The greatest contribution that the Christian church has given to Western civilization is the transmission of ideas from the Hebrew tradition. However, even as the Hebrews would become corrupted by materialism and positivism, expressed through idols and rituals, so Western Christianity had become tainted with a reverence for modern science, particularly higher criticism and psychology. The home school has the opportunity to restore pure education by having students concentrate on subjects that are di-

7. The Curriculum: The Means of Pure Education

vergent, rather than convergent. Charles Darwin lost his heart, his soul, and his mind by changing divergent knowledge into convergent solutions through *reductionism*. Knowledge concerning man, life, and death cannot be reduced merely as solutions that are either "right" or "wrong." However, according to the reductionist, man is nothing but a higher form of ape, life is nothing but the result of the "accidental collocations of atoms," and death is nothing but the cessation of existence. Therefore, no one should wonder why children are killing children in the public schools.

08 THE CURRICULUM
Enriching the Heart with the Bible

No one can attain to a strong and idiomatic prose style or be able to appreciate fully the masterpieces of English literature without a constant study of the English Bible.

—Fred Lewis Pattee, *The Foundations of English Literature*

And that from a child thou hast known the holy scriptures, which are able to make thee wise unto salvation through faith which is in Christ Jesus.

—2 Timothy 3:15

Perhaps the one enigma that puzzles students of the Gospels the most is how the Hebrew scribes could have missed the Messiah. The scribes were dedicated to preserving the Hebrew culture by copying the various documents of Judaism, including the sacred writings known as the Old Testament. An elaborate procedure for copying was developed, and the checks for accuracy were strictly observed, because the scribes believed that they were handling the very words of God. In fact, the scribes knew the Scriptures well enough to tell Herod where Christ was to be born. Yet during his ministry, Jesus Christ vehemently denounced these men and poured the most heated invectives upon them, even more than upon the regimes of Herod and Rome. As for their attitude toward Jesus Christ, the scribes had a mutual hatred toward Him, even to the point of plotting to kill Him. The scribes offer the best example of the consequence awaiting men and women who possess merely an intellectual knowledge of the Bible. Even though they knew the Scriptures, the scribes failed to know God. The Bible is to be applied not to the intellect but to the heart. Therefore, if they are to enrich others with grace and wisdom, students must carefully guard their hearts with the Bible.

If they reject the Bible, secularists must seek a non-religious guide by which to guard their hearts. While Emerson would do well, perhaps the writings of Benjamin Franklin would be even better. His *Autobiography* is delightful, witty, and thought-provoking. Even though he was raised a Presbyterian, Franklin seldom attended church services. On the occasions that he did, Franklin found the preaching to be "very dry, uninteresting, and unedifying, since not a single moral principle was inculcated or enforc'd." According to Franklin, the purpose of this dryness was to create good Presbyterians rather than "good citizens." After rejecting the established church, Franklin sets out on his own "bold and arduous project of arriving at moral perfection." Adopting Plato's idea of developing good habits, Franklin convinced himself that by replacing bad habits with good ones, individuals could perfect themselves morally. Franklin lists thirteen virtues, which he would conscientiously apply to his own life. The thirteenth virtue is humility,

8. The Curriculum: Enriching the Heart with the Bible

which according to Franklin was the imitation of Jesus and Socrates. One who is bold enough to attempt his own moral perfection may find humility a bit hard to muster. Nevertheless, if they were to follow Franklin's thirteen virtues, individuals would no doubt become good people, whom most people would welcome as their next-door neighbors.

But like any philosopher who tries to use human reason to develop a system of morals, Franklin discovers the heart to be treacherous: "But I soon found I had undertaken a task of more difficulty than I had imagined. While my care was employ'd in guarding against one fault, I was often surprised by another."

Such is the human condition, because "the heart is deceitful above all things, and desperately wicked: who can know it?" (Jeremiah 17:9). Fortunately, man is not left to ponder this question philosophically, since the next verse begins with "I the LORD search the heart" (verse 10). Since the Western tradition rejects the concept of sin and believes that evil is the result of bad habits, most public educators think the answer to society's troubles is just more education. Whatever the bad habit is at the time, whether cigarette smoking, chastity, or Christianity, the solution will always be more education, or in other words, more taxes, more bureaucrats, and more oppression. But as the Hebrew tradition has made clear to Western civilization, it is hearts that need transforming, not everyone's habits.

It cannot be emphasized enough that the most important possession that students own is their hearts. The heart is the seat for both thought and emotions by which students will reveal their true selves. While students may not be able to know their hearts, they certainly can know about their hearts. The Holy Bible of 1611, commonly known as the Authorized King James Version, refers to the heart 953 times. The first mention of the heart is in Genesis 6:5, in connection with the thoughts of the heart being continually evil. The last mention of the heart is in Revelation 18:7 concerning the heart of Mystery Babylon, whose affections center on buying and selling, merchandising in everything from gold to the souls of men, which are regarded as cheap.

Throughout the Scriptures, the unregenerate heart is depicted as unworthy of trust and as an unreliable guide for determining thoughts and affections. Thus, pure education must deal with the heart first. If their hearts are not guarded daily from perverseness, then regardless whether students read incessantly from the ancient and modern classics, know five languages, and write poetry like a Tennyson or compose novels like a Dickens, students will have a perverted view of life, centered on themselves and perceived as an array of contradictions and strife, like Romeo believed when he declared, "O brawling love! O loving hate!" Students need a guidebook for their heart, and this guidebook must prove to be reliable, powerful, and timeless.

One question that I generally use for final examinations in my beginning composition classes has the central idea of rescuing books from destruction due to a radical change in society, whether by shipwreck or by tyranny. The students are asked if they knew that they could have only three books to read for the rest of their lives, what three books would they choose, and why. I instruct the students to give reasons why these particular books will help them now and for future generations later, when these books are passed on to others.

8. The Curriculum: Enriching the Heart with the Bible

I have yet to see a student wanting the works of Plato, Aristotle, Descartes, or Hume. In addition to this, no student has mentioned a single book about mathematics or science. On the other hand, even though works by Homer, Dickens, and Shakespeare rank very high on the list of favorites, the indisputable choice that 95 percent of students in my classes want to preserve is the Bible. One would expect this result to be true at a Christian college, but these students are products of the public schools and are students at a state college. In spite of the "bad press" about the Bible, when life gets down to the bare essentials, when getting a good job is no longer a concern, and when buying unnecessary things is a thing of the past, the Bible becomes the first choice among those who wish to know something about living.

Now, let me change the question for the home educator. If—for whatever reason—you were allowed to have only one book at your disposal for educating your students, what book would you choose to be worthy enough to be given to the next generation? Undoubtedly, like the composition students, the Bible would become the choice of home educators. The Bible is complete with history, with heartwarming stories about love, bravery, and devotion, and with words of unmatched wisdom. Between its covers, the Bible has the finest poetry in the world, the most excellent drama, and the most profound philosophical presentations. Above all, men and women are told how they can reconcile themselves to God. When Professor Pattee taught and wrote 140 years ago, the word *Bible* was not misunderstood by anyone. However, *Bible* is so vague today that it has become a meaningless word unless qualified. Therefore, a follow-up question is required for the home educator: "*Which* Bible would you choose?"

The answer is a reasonable one today because of the multifarious versions of the Bible available. For nearly three hundred years, the people of the English-speaking world had but one Bible. But the twentieth century, with its rampant industrialism, saw a proliferation of books calling themselves Bibles. In spite of the pious reasons for the publishing of the different versions, one has to suspect the love of money to be the leading motive behind the publications. Unfortunately, industrialism has not only infected American Christianity with the overproduction of "new and improved" Bibles, but commercialism has cheapened the roles of music and benevolence in the churches as well.

Few would bother with the professional "Christian" musicians and beggars if it were not for the sanctified sales force dedicated to hard selling the Christian public to buy their products and to support their ministries. Whether in a pulpit, in a magazine, or on television, advertising has the sole purpose of inciting lust in consumers to buy something they do not need. Being gullible suckers—according to P. T. Barnum—Christian Americans buy the latest Christian symbol, book, or music, because they have been conditioned to accept anything new and reject anything old. Unfortunately for the churches, this "new is better" mentality is a thief and a robber—a thief of values and a robber of culture.

Which Bible should students use to guard their hearts? From a literary and cultural point of view, the Holy Bible of 1611 stands supreme. The superiority of the Authorized Version is attested to the fact that this book remains the standard by which *every* new translation of the Scriptures is forced to be measured. New translations have come and gone: Revised Version, American Standard Version, and the Revised Standard Version are just a few. Of course,

8. The Curriculum: Enriching the Heart with the Bible

it is very possible that the expiration of the copyrights might have led to the demise of these versions. In order to keep the money coming in, the publishers introduced a *New* American Standard Version and a *New* Revised Standard Version. If history is a reliable indication of the future, then Christians can expect an *Improved* New International Version several years from now.

Not only is the Authorized Version still the standard for all Bibles, but this book also continues to have the presumption as being the best of all Bibles available today. Even the editors at Zondervan remark in the *NIV / KJV Parallel Bible* that the Authorized Version will remain a blessing at the present time and in the future because of its elevated English style. Since the teacher should use only the best materials to educate her students, this fact alone should settle the answer concerning the Bible to be used in the home school.

However, there are other compelling reasons for the student to use the Authorized Version. This Bible was not a translation from scratch. Technically, the Authorized Version is a revision of William Tyndale's New Testament and Myles Coverdale's Old Testament. The Matthew, Great, Bishop, and Geneva Bibles were refinements of the Tyndale-Coverdale's Bible, which the Authorized Version finalized eighty-six years later. During these years, England became "the people of a book." Tyndale provided the vision at the cost of his life; the other men provided enrichment and harmony to Tyndale's words. The fifty-four scholars of the Authorized Version were divided into three committees for a total of six companies, which were responsible for different portions of the Scriptures. Each scholar would work independently on his assignment, comparing other translations and offering his own translation only if deemed necessary. The company would then meet to discuss the relative merits of the various passages. Only after there was a consensus to the English words did the panel approve the selection. At this point, the work was reviewed by the other companies. With all of these scholars reviewing the work, the Authorized Version lacks the peculiarities of the previous versions of the Bible. Because no single piece of literature can claim a more wondrous story than the development of the Authorized Version, the student should become acquainted with the history of the English Bible. The lessons taught about devotion, sacrifice, and courage are without equal.

Not only is the Authorized Version the product of very careful scholarship, but the version is also the easiest Bible to understand. Modern publishers claim that their versions are easier to read and to understand than the Authorized Version. Yet how "Negev," "Magi," and "miraculous signs" are easier to understand than "the south," "wise men," and "miracles" exceeds the reader's credulity.

Perhaps the biggest complaint against the Authorized Version is the use of *thou* and *ye*. In the introduction of an early edition of the New International Version, the committee makes a point to justify its exclusion of these "archaisms," which gives pause for wondering why justification for removing any antiquated and inapplicable words is necessary at all. According to the scholars, *Thou* as a specific pronoun for God does not exist in the ancient languages. Also, the scholars insist the forms of *thou* and *ye* do not clarify anything today, even though these expressions apparently were a part of everyday conversion in the seventeenth century.

The NIV translators committed several errors here. First, while the ancient languages did not use particular pronouns for divinity, neither does the English in the Authorized Version. The so-

8. The Curriculum: Enriching the Heart with the Bible

called special pronouns are used in the same manner for *both* God and men. Therefore, violation of accuracy is not a concern. Second, a present-day version would be indeed "enhanced" by the English of 1611. Otherwise, why is the note for John 3:7 (NIV) necessary for the reader to know that this pronoun is plural? The word *ye* would have made the note unnecessary. And last, those living in England in 1611 did not use the familiar form of the second person on a daily basis.

As a matter of fact, the familiar forms of the second person are used primarily in poetry, which means the Authorized Version is written in an *elevated language*, the mark of all great literature. The familiar forms of second person pronouns are the singular *thou* (*thee, thy*) and the plural *ye* (*you, your*). *Thou* connotes an intimate relationship. The formal forms of the word *you* (*you, your*) in the second person was an address used to express a distant respect. The formal and familiar forms of the second person are not unique in English; they appear also in Spanish with the formal *usted* and *ustedes* and the familiar *tú* and *vosotros*.

By employing exclusively the second person in its familiar form, the scholars of the Authorized Version clarified the understanding of the Scriptures. Anyone who reads the Ten Commandments in the New International Version could wonder whether the commandments are to the reader personally or to the collective. The reason why there is no doubt about the commandments being individually applied is because the Authorized Version has already helped the other Bible out. A good example of real confusion is in the rendering of the NIV passage of John 3:1–15. Jesus switches from speaking with Nicodemus to addressing several listeners. But without the English familiar forms, the reader would never have known this.

Interestingly, in the dedication to the king, the translators address King James as "you." As mentioned already, *you* means a distant respect; *thou* shows a close intimacy. While students should develop a relationship of respect for God, it is more important to cultivate a special intimacy with their heavenly Father. *Thou* is the better address. If the scholarship of the NIV translators is such that they completely misunderstood the use of the English familiar form of the second person as it applied to the Authorized Version, one should wonder if these many scholars were careless or ignorant elsewhere.

Those with any literary taste whatsoever recognize the Authorized Version as the greatest literary work in the English language, and many have even argued it is the best in the world. On the other hand, the modern versions cannot claim to be part of the belles lettres, because they either did not or have not yet survived the test of time, and they all fail to use an elevated language and a superior crafting of words to express ideas. Not only has the Authorized Version endured the test of time, but it has also withstood innumerable criticisms beginning with Hugh Broughton, a scholar who was not invited to join the translators due to his arrogance and self-pride. In 1611, after reviewing the Authorized Version, Broughton wrote, "The new edition crosseth me. I require it to be burnt." Broughton died in 1612.

Not only do the current versions lack the test of time, but also modern translators are too concerned with the sense of the words and not with the sound of them. The moment translators become more concerned about pedantry and about putting the Scriptures into the language of the street, they have automatically doomed their version to obscurity along with all other cheap literature.

8. The Curriculum: Enriching the Heart with the Bible

While abundant evidence exists today for the deterioration of the English language, the times of Queen Elizabeth and King James were immersed in poetry. Edmund Spenser, Ben Jonson, Christopher Marlowe, John Donne, and William Shakespeare were household names. From the meanest to the highest stations in life, everyone was thinking, speaking, and writing poetically.

To the English poet, sounds, syntax, and stress are paramount. Not being poets, modern translators fail to appreciate these qualities. For example, in the New International Version, one finds, "I speak the truth in Christ—I am not lying, my conscience confirms it through the Holy Spirit" (Romans 9:1). The words *speak, conscience, confirms*, and *Spirit* overload the verse with too many harsh sounds. Even though the beginning of the verse with three iambs is admirable, the translators merely borrowed the syntax and rhythm from the Authorized Version. The phrase *I am not lying* is insipid and fails to provide any emphasis, which Paul intends in the passage.

However, the Authorized Version states, "I say the truth in Christ, I lie not, my conscience also bearing me witness in the Holy Ghost." Here the verse is softened with the long vowel sounds of *say, lie, me*, and *Holy Ghost*. Regarding its rhythm, the verse begins with three iambs, and the clause "I lie not," because of its syntax, requires a stress on all three words, which provides the desired emphasis on all three syllables. Notice also the assonance of "Christ, I lie."

Every line of the Authorized Version has these rhythms and wordsmanship. The anapests and iambs found in Romans 6:23 and the anapests used in Isaiah 53:1 are not the result of an accident. Lancelot Andrews, a personal friend of Edmund Spenser, is credited with much of the cadence found in the Authorized Version. It is the cadence that aids in public reading and with memorization of the Scriptures. This attention to sounds, syntax, and rhythm in the Authorized Version makes the entire work not one of prose but rather one of poetry, known as *free verse*. Arguably, it was the scholars of the Authorized Version who originated free verse, not Walt Whitman, who is often credited with creating the form. Like Whitman, if the modern versions happen to have a good rhythm or syntax, it is because the words and cadence were borrowed from the Authorized Version.

Another mark of great literature is that the work lends itself to rereading, because the message is timeless, appealing to all generations, young and old. With each rereading, the reader *always* learns something new. This is true because the reader has experienced more of life with each subsequent reading. How so very true this is regarding the Holy Bible, which millions of souls have searched daily to find comfort, joy, and peace. Promises are found and claimed, and instruction in righteousness is received. All great literature elevates the soul. How much more can the soul be elevated than to be blessed "with all spiritual blessings in heavenly places in Christ" (Eph. 1:3)?

What is the conclusion of the matter? In short, time has proven that modern Christians in America have never needed a "new" Bible. For over a hundred years, ignoble attempts accompanied by massive advertising have been made to replace the Authorized Version. In reality, American "Bibles" are not translations at all, because the editors do not offer a word-for-word translation of the original languages. They prefer getting the "gist of the idea." Thus, what the market is flooded with are interpretations, not transla-

8. The Curriculum: Enriching the Heart with the Bible

tions. How a passage is interpreted is the prerogative between the reader and the Holy Spirit of God, and no one else.

Therefore, scholars, committees, and publishers have been unable to improve upon the Authorized Version—and they never will. The decline in the appreciation of the English language ensures their failure. For the home educator who desires to offer the best education to her students, the Authorized Version becomes historically significant, because it represents the single book that ended the foundational stage of modern English by preserving the best of the English language. The language needed a vehicle to standardize the spellings and structures found in English. It was the reading of the Holy Bible of 1611 by the light of millions of candles and fireplaces that educated the young and the old, promoted the ideas of liberty, lead thousands of missionaries around the world, and established the unique American institution of the Christian liberal arts college. The beginning of this Bible was baptized in the blood of William Tyndale and ended with the poetic genius of scholars who were second to none during their lifetime—or since then. As more Americans lightly toss aside the Authorized Version as irrelevant for today's student, the nation will continue to experience consequences disastrous not only to the hearts of its students but to the heritage of its citizens as well.

May it not be said of home educators that they chose poorly.

09 THE CURRICULUM
Enriching the Soul with Literature

> *Who kills a man kills a reasonable creature, God's image; but he who destroys a good book, kills reason itself, kills the image of God, as it were in the eye.*
>
> —JOHN MILTON, *Areopagitica*

> *The cloke that I left at Troas with Carpus, when thou comest, bring with thee, and the books, but especially the parchments.*
>
> —2 TIMOTHY 4:13

If wishing to witness the vanity of human desire to be immortal in this life, one merely needs to visit the local library. On the many shelves sit books by authors—scholars, poets, novelists, and others—who have been long forgotten, along with their ideas. It is not that these writers failed to have anything worthwhile to say. Perhaps Seneca expressed it best when he stated many years ago, *Otium sine litteris mors est et hominis vivi sepultura*, or "Leisure without literature is death, or rather the burial of a living man." Americans have redefined leisure to exclude intellectual activity, and therefore they have truly buried themselves alive. For next to preparing the heart, pure education prepares the soul, and nothing affects the soul more than the pursuit of literature.

For the purposes of this chapter, literature includes languages, both modern and ancient, philosophy, history, and belles lettres. To be an educated person is to be a devotee of literature. Undoubtedly, the concept of the core curriculum causes the greatest harm in the field of literature. Ancient languages have been dropped as irrelevant, philosophy is viewed as unimportant, history is rejected as a fine art, and classical, American, and British literature are considered for the most part dead letters. Some college professors even contend that a study of the lyrics in songs by Paul McCartney and Madonna are more valuable today than Homer and Shakespeare.

Yet even if all of the above subjects under literature were offered in a school, the courses would be so fragmented and so compartmentalized that a student would fail to perceive the connection between Dickens's novel *Hard Times* and Mill's *Utilitarianism,* or between the historical Descartes and Cartesian geometry in mathematics. In other words, the modern educational system has eliminated the single-most important vehicle that nourishes the soul. If one wonders why most Americans seem to lack purpose, then the wonder stops here. The central discipline that makes education different from technical training is missing in the schools.

Any discussion about literature must begin with language. It should be axiomatic that a student that is incapable of using a language in order to read well will be a dull student indeed. Yet millions of high school graduates are not sufficiently prepared to

9. The Curriculum: Enriching the Soul with Literature

do college work precisely because they read with little comprehension. Colleges and universities have attempted to remedy the situation by offering "developmental studies" in writing and reading. Yet, in spite of these programs, when asked what they had just read, it is still all too common for college students who had read out loud a portion from the *Iliad* to answer, "I don't know; I just read."

For the most part, college professors are perplexed by the growing trend among students who refuse to read their assignments. However, if students "just read," but do not know what they are reading, then reading is surely a colossal waste of time. Even if the professors are puzzled, the students themselves are not in the least. New college students discover immediately that they were not trained to read. Technically trained students do not read books; only educated people do. When college freshmen are asked what skills their high school teachers failed to give them, the two complaints that lead the list are *proper study skills* and *requiring more reading*. There is a feeling among first-year college students that they were cheated somehow. On the other hand, these young people cannot understand why a college professor gets angry when the entire class is unable to explain the difference between *capitalism* and *socialism*. Of course, these ideas are unimportant for future corporate or governmental workers, who can get a job regardless of the economic system under which they work.

If the goal of the student is to get a job, then a good vocabulary is not absolutely necessary. However, any high school student who has ever taken a college entrance exam realizes that someone thinks a good vocabulary is important. Words like *parsimonious, propitious,* and *vex* are not common words today, but these words are quite common on the SAT and in classical literature. When students are admitted to college, they should possess a better-than-average vocabulary. But a good working vocabulary can be learned only by a constant reading of quality literature, which uses an elevated vocabulary. Reading any current novel or newspaper merely offends the sensibilities of educated people, who feel that their time can be better employed elsewhere. The so-called modern literature is seldom uplifting, not only because the novels and poetry have such dismal themes, but also because they are written in the language of the drunkard in the barroom.

Therefore, literature—in order to be called literature—must have elevated ideas, expressed with elevated words. But what are *words*? In reality, a word is simply a symbol that represents an idea, which in turn is packed with meaning. For an example, the word *fog* has its literal, or scientific, meaning and its figurative, or imaginary, meaning. A *fog* is condensed water vapor in cloud-like masses lying close to the ground and limiting visibility. On the other hand, a *fog* can be a mental vagueness or confusion. All of this is very fine, except for one problem: a word by itself is meaningless. If the word *fog* is removed for the context of other words, then no one can know for certain what the intended meaning of the word is. Thus, knowledge of a language is important, and a mark of the educated person is a good vocabulary, and from the educated vocabulary comes the symbols, which convey greater and clearer meaning. It is a shame that the best some public schools could do for a slogan was "Because I got somebody to be." If our future leaders of America can muster only ideas like "Hey dude, that's awesome," or "Got whatever?" then God help us.

At the age of five, children have learned a lot of words by merely imitating the speech and syntax of speakers, particularly

9. The Curriculum: Enriching the Soul with Literature

their parents. The early instruction in reading and vocabulary is primarily to prepare the student to read more difficult material later. For this reason, the only valid reason for learning ancient languages is to prepare the student to read the ancient works in Greek or Latin. Many educators suggest that Greek and Latin aid a student with English vocabulary. Perhaps this is true. But why should a student learn conjugations of verbs and declension of nouns in order to build his English vocabulary? Other teachers espouse the belief that ancient languages help the student to understand English grammar better. Yet one wonders how *urbem pugnabamus defendere* [we were fighting to defend the city] will help a student to learn the lesson that good rhetorical writing will have subjects preceding verbs and their adverbs.

Young men went to grammar schools to learn the Latin language so that they could later study Virgil, Cicero, and other Latin poets and writers. As part of his entrance exam to Franklin College, Alexander Stephens had to read from a Roman author as assigned by the examiner. When he heard that he would have to read from Cicero, Stephens felt a growing panic. He had prepared for the most probable readings—all except for Cicero. Finally, Stephens was asked to read on a certain page from the book. To his relief, the passage was the only one with which Stephens was very familiar, because he was drawn to this particular passage. Cicero had expressed his views on capital punishment in the passage, which Stephens thought to have been very interesting when he studied this portion in grammar school. Since many of the ancient works were not translated into English, students, if they hoped to be educated, had to know Greek and Latin in order to benefit from the writings coming from ancient Greece and Rome.

However, today most ancient works are available in adequate translations. Is there still any justification to learning Latin or Greek? Yes, there is. Eliminating the ancient classics, or even translating them, has robbed students of the personality and of the originality of Homer, Virgil, Cato, Cicero, and other ancient writers. The loss of the author's words, though other symbols may be adequate, is a separation of the soul from the work. The student no longer admires the words of the author but rather the words of the translator. Horace in English would be the same as Shakespeare in German. The translations no longer represent the words or the beauty of Horace or Shakespeare. Without reading Virgil in the Latin tongue, the student may still know about the *Aeneid*, but he will fail to achieve a meeting of the mind with the great Roman poet himself. While reading "All of Gaul is divided into three parts" may give the gist of the idea, to truly connect with Julius Caesar mentally, students need to read *"Gallia est omnis divisi en tres partes."* In her "Sonnet I," Elizabeth Barrett Browning reflects upon a poem by Theocritus by which she was transported back into her past:

> *And, as I mused it in his antique tongue,*
> *I saw, in gradual vision through my tears*
> *The sweet, sad years, the melancholy years,*
> *Those of my own life, who by turns had flung*
> *A shadow across me.*

Browning contemplated the words of Theocritus in Greek, thereby touching her soul with his soul. This poem moved her emotions, and such is the noble office of literature. In American education, it is this loss of continuity with the past that has become

9. The Curriculum: Enriching the Soul with Literature

so grievous and that has destroyed the touching of modern souls with ancient ones. But according to modern educators, the loss is not a great one. Unless something helps the student to get a job, today's teachers merely tolerate, if not ignore, anything that tends to elevate a student's character, emotions, and soul.

The home school student should learn well at least one ancient language. If the student is to learn but one ancient language, that language ought to be Latin. While classical Greek has value, Latin is better, because the language is more difficult to master. Students should be encouraged to tackle the tough things in life as a matter of fact. But, more important, there are a greater number of books and poems for the student's perusal written in Latin than in Greek. The reason for these many works is because Latin was the language of the educated man for nearly 1,600 years. Only since 1650 have the modern languages dethroned Latin as the language of learning. Francis Bacon believed that Latin would always remain the language of the educated; therefore, all of his scholarly studies were written in Latin, not English. Bacon thought that his works in Latin would be preserved forever for scholars and students in the future. Unfortunately, while Bacon was a brilliant thinker, he was no prophet.

Since they should have a good knowledge of language by the eighth grade, students should begin studies in Greek or Latin as soon as possible—in fact, the sooner, the better. John Stuart Mill was home educated by his father, who started John's studies in Greek at the age of three and in Latin at the age of eight. Regarding modern languages, the purpose for learning a language is the same as for English and ancient languages: the student should be able to read a nation's literature in the native language. Of the many languages to study, the student would be wise to study either French or German. One of the long-term goals of the student is to earn a graduate degree. It is hoped that the student under pure education will pursue literature, philosophy, or history in graduate school, which will require the student to have a proficiency in French or German. Remember, language is imitation; therefore, the learning of ancient and foreign languages should be a family affair and the languages should be spoken in the home as much as possible.

The greatest casualty in modern education concerns the study of history. Before the 1900s, history was included under literature. The father of history, Herodotus, believed that the purpose for writing histories should be for preserving the past, or "in order that the things men have done might not in time be forgotten." Herodotus's statement implies that "the things men have done" should be preserved for all to remember, scholars and common men together. Not too long ago, histories were indeed written for the general reading public. Dickens, Carlyle, and Gibbon wrote histories that rivaled the best novels of their day. But at the beginning of the twentieth century, historians became scientific with their presentation of history. Data were collected, analyzed, and listed by the scientists, and the histories essentially belonged to the insiders of the brotherhood of historians. The writing of history was no longer an art that attempted to appeal to the common man. If a few outsiders happened to receive some enlightenment, that was fine, but for the most part, historical discussions remained in scholarly journals, which is still true today.

However, even though some authors are trying to revive history as literature, like Simon Jenkins and John Man (*A Short History of England* and *Saladin*, respectively), the study of history in

9. The Curriculum: Enriching the Soul with Literature

the schools is now consigned to textbooks containing subjectively selected facts, which the student has to memorize and regurgitate on tests. The result of this fact-oriented approach to history has been tragic, because students receive the wrong impression about the meaning and purpose of history.

The scientific approach to history suggests that there is a finality with the facts. However, no history is ever finished. While some philosophers state that the writing of history is one of evolution, a better term would be one of continuous inspiration. A historian may write a history of the United States that is very broad, but another historian may want to concentrate on the War for American Independence. Still another historian may center on writing about the Continental army and its battles. Then again, some scholar may write a book on the battle of Yorktown. And maybe three or four historians may write about this particular battle, giving their own unique view of the events that led to the battle.

The point here is that the past has two parts. The first part is the moment when choices were made, and these choices cannot be altered once they have taken place. The events happened and are now forever suspended without further motion. On the other hand, the interpretation of the choices that led to the events forever lives, because inspiration and imagination add to the history at any point in time. No one can be an objective observer whenever participating in the present, such as the soldier scaling a redoubt at Yorktown. Histories can only be written after a passing of time. One history leads to the writing of another history, and yet another. Ideally, histories ought to help the student to pity and correct the mistakes made by many, to grieve at injustice of all, and to rejoice in the successes of others. Thus, the reading of history should stir the emotions first, and then the intellect.

But if students merely know that the Normans conquered England in 1066, that Columbus discovered the New World in 1492, and that Pearl Harbor was bombed on December 7, 1941, then they have learned a chronological list, but they have not learned any history. The tedium of lists with names, dates, and events that are separated from their contexts has caused students to dislike the study of history—falsely so called. While there was a "real" Julius Caesar, who is dead and gone, the historical Julius Caesar is immortal, who lives in histories and other literature. The student can even read Caesar's own account in Latin of the Gallic wars in the *Commentaries*, through which the student becomes intimately acquainted with one of the greatest military and political figures of the past. The student can even feel pity for Caesar as seen through the eyes of William Shakespeare in his *Tragedy of Julius Caesar*. Through literature, the historical Caesar is revealed and lives; in the textbook, it is best not to praise Caesar, but to bury him.

Regarding the literature under history, the home school student should read as many original sources as possible. The Bible should not be ignored as a source of ancient history. Autobiographies and biographies are excellent literature, particularly if the men and women are worthy of imitation. Diaries of individuals such as Mary Chestnut's *Dairy from Dixie* are better than reading a book of criticism on her book, although the criticism may be valuable as well. Historical novels are good, so long as the student realizes that some of the events may be fictitious. However, the value of the historical novel rests in its ability to present history in a delightful way. The student may be prompted to read other books concerning the events and setting surrounding the novel. For an example, Dickens's *A Tale of Two Cities* might be followed with

9. The Curriculum: Enriching the Soul with Literature

reading Thomas Carlyle's *French Revolution* and Edmund Burke's *Reflections on the Revolution in France*. In short, one history ought to lead the student to read another history. But every history will be tainted with self-interest and subjectivity. This is also true with diaries. If the only source that researchers will have two hundred years from now were the *New York Times*, what will the historians actually know about the people of the United States, much less the common man who reports to a job every morning? All writers look at the events past and present with their own perceptions and assumptions. However, a reading of several sources about the same event allows students to form their own judgments and opinions. Since editors are very selective with material, this subjectivity is why textbooks are inadequate for teaching history.

The chief ends of literature, particularly the belles lettres, are two-fold. First, the primary end for reading the belles lettres is to delight the soul of the student, which is the purpose of all art. In the industrialized schools of America, literature courses are mechanical, with the student memorizing insignificant tidbits about the plot of a work or author. The great issues of life regarding a character's struggle with right or wrong, or the tragic hero's flaw causing his downfall, may be alluded to but never fully developed or discussed. However, the truth of the matter is that literature cannot be taught. Since literature is a form of art, a home educator can teach *about* literature, but she cannot *teach* literature. Literature exists as an art, because the adequate expression of literature is impossible in any other form. In the pages of literature, the soul is touched, the emotions are stirred, and the mind reflects on beauty. Therefore, students do not learn literature; they must experience it. If the student fails to read the works of Homer or John Keats, then it is impossible to discover and receive delight in the beauty found in the words of these poets. So it is true with all works of literature.

Another important end to literature is to provide ideas for the student. At first, these ideas are in the form of words, the self-contained symbols used for self-expression. The mind should master the words; indeed, the words must not enslave the mind. The student who can recite, "Thomas Gray belonged to the Graveyard Poets," but is unable to explain the significance of Gray's poetry is a slave to words. In addition to appreciating the power of words, the student is directly responsible for learning about life. A teacher can direct the student and should be an example worthy of emulation, but students must in the end experience their own lives and form their own thoughts.

Perhaps for this reason, it is difficult to get some students to sit still long enough to read a book. Life is new, and there is much to discover. The emphasis with the young person is the present; the past is for old people to reflect about. Yet this is the perfect time to cultivate a taste for reading. Young people are governed generally by their emotions and feelings. Therefore, literature is the best source to direct and guide the student when experiencing love, anger, bitterness, or any other emotion. Whether directed or not, students will imitate something; this something ought to be the best of all ideas.

Ideas require thinking, and governmental officials tend to be paranoid about the thinking individual. When Caesar says concerning Cassius, "He thinks too much: such men are dangerous," Shakespeare is acknowledging the fact that a thinking people will always be a danger to tyranny and corrupt government. Judge Robert Bork was denied a seat on the U.S. Supreme Court not because he was

9. The Curriculum: Enriching the Soul with Literature

incompetent, but because he wrote too much. Bork's ideas were dangerous to the established powers. Unfortunately, the lesson learned by the U.S. Senate's action in the case of Judge Bork is that if candidates desire to pursue any high office in the corrupt halls of government, they better not write about their thoughts, nor should they ever let their thoughts be scrutinized by the public at all. On the other hand, wholesome government welcomes and encourages those who manipulate ideas. While this freedom may allow some to embrace error, people of character and of ideas welcome the dissent, because their convictions are tested by error.

However, this testing is due not to individuals doubting their positions, but to their confident belief in the truth of their ideas. The free individual is confident that error when compared to the truth will be clearly manifested for what it is. For this reason, the Bible is repressed in public life not because of its religious nature but because of its being literature that expresses irrefutable ideas about truth. Crooks and charlatans want nothing to disturb their successful con game. The reading of literature always generates ideas, particularly when those ideas come from the classical works, which represent the best and noblest examples of thinking by humankind. If the home-school movement is attacked in the future by the national and state governments, the reason will be not because the home schools are failing but because these schools are proving to be too successful by producing thinkers.

10 THE CURRICULUM
Enriching the Soul with Art and Music

If you get simple beauty and nought else,
You get about the best thing God invents.

—ROBERT BROWNING, *"Fra Lippo Lippi"*

Out of Zion, the perfection of beauty, God hath shined.

—PSALM 50:2

In the United States, beauty is an endangered species. When one considers a poem, a painting, a symphony, a statue, and an ancient Greek structure, a common trait among these various expressions of human endeavor does not seem to emerge at first. Also, when anyone makes a judgment that this painting is a good work of art, but that one is a poor example, what is the criterion? Are tastes in music merely subjective, where one listener prefers heavy metal, while another prefers classical music, and both are equally valid? One would think so. Art as being "in the eye [or ear] of the beholder" has become so commonplace that most Americans accept this adage as an everlasting maxim. Many years ago, when a firestorm of protest erupted over the public display of a photograph showing a crucifix in a glass of supposed urine, arguments filled the newspapers for allowing artists the freedom to exercise their artistic expressions. Counterarguments attacked the photograph's content as "disgusting," "inappropriate," and "offensive." However, if the crucifix were in a glass of sweet tea, would the photograph now be respectable? Other arguments conceded the privilege of the artist to express himself as he sees fit, but not at taxpayers' expense. But as usual, the central issue was never discussed. The unanswered question is whether this photograph represents art in the first place.

As a philosophical study, aesthetics began in the eighteenth century as part of the social movement called *modernism*. Because modernism has its roots in evolutionary theory, the traditional view of aesthetics begins poorly. Modernism posits both the progress in the arts, which builds on the past, and artists who actively work for social change through their art. Since art is evolving, it is not surprising that critics believe that art is constantly progressing forward. However, this progress is often not toward greater clarification, but regretfully toward greater abstraction.

On the other hand, *postmodernism* rejects the above view. Whereas modernists assert evolution, postmodernists embrace subjectivity. According to the postmodernists, the history of art does not show a line of progression, but rather a coexistence of several kinds of art. Therefore, to prefer one expression of art over another is meaningless, because the art can be applicable only in its cultural setting. In this case, objective standards do not exist to determine the value of any art. For the postmodernists, the reason

10. The Curriculum: Enriching the Soul with Art and Music

why some art is preferred by society over another kind is because of a dominant group repressing alternative expressions of art, of which the power elite disapproves.

Of course, the positions of both the modernist and the postmodernist are unsatisfactory for defining art. While on the one hand art and music are at the mercy of a materialistic determinism, the arts become nonexistent on the other hand, because a painting by Monet would be no better than a teenager's graffiti on the wall of a subway. As the modern philosophers wrangle over the definition of art, most people instinctively believe that art is connected with whatever is beautiful. What the philosophers fail to understand is that beauty is not a quality; therefore, it falls outside of the realm of the intellect, thereby defying logic and making most philosophical conclusions about art hopelessly deficient. Beauty is an effect that touches the emotions; thus, art affects the soul, not the mind. Art is to be experienced, not intellectually manipulated.

According to the Hebrews, to whom the West must turn for its ideas, the expression of art is the soul striving for perfection, even though this perfection is unattainable in this present world. Of course, this definition presupposes that absolute perfection exists to act as an objective standard to measure this drive toward perfection. For this reason, sensitive souls have not only tried to preserve the beautiful found in their cultures, but they have also appreciated the beautiful both in the past and in the present. The source of beauty is God as manifested in His creation. Therefore, artists do not create in the sense of producing anything *ex nihilo*, but they duplicate that which is already perfect. Whenever the artist paints a landscape, the poet writes a poem, and the composer creates a concerto, they attempt to capture an experience that is beautiful with existing colors, words, or sounds, hoping to suspend the experience in time. The artist, poet, and composer will be successful only if they express well the sublimity of the moment, using materials found in nature. A painter cannot create a new color, nor can a composer produce a new note. For this reason, the key phrase for legitimate art is *imitation of nature*.

Therefore, true artistic genius tries to duplicate nature, not the works of other men. Many tyros aspire to be great, but the best that most will ever achieve is producing a mediocre imitation of an artistic genius, who was directly sensitive with the beauty in nature. Nevertheless, the imitation of genius is a necessary step toward greatness. Of course, to aspire to be great will often prove to be disappointing. Great personalities of the past never sought fame; their greatness resulted from their giving to others something of value. Jesus Christ expresses this paradox best by declaring the first will be last and the last will be first. If students wish to provide something valuable to their culture, they must humble themselves first to imitate the best before them, and then, if their souls are sensitive enough, they will discover their own unique imitation of nature. Therefore, true artists are rare in human history, because they are givers, not takers. Great painters, greater writers, and great musicians are immortal, because their works touch the souls of all for subsequent generations, allowing fellow human beings to share a beautiful and sublime moment uniquely experienced by the artist.

But as shown before, modern America is at war with nature and culture. Technology and science wish not to imitate nature but rather to conquer and reform it. The landscape is stripped of its trees and soil for minerals, while junk vehicles litter the landscape across the country. Overproduction of tillable soil and attempts to

10. The Curriculum: Enriching the Soul with Art and Music

increase yields by using insecticides, herbicides, and fungicides provide unsafe food for a population plagued with homicides, infanticides, and suicides. Writers, musicians, and painters produce shallow plots, pitiful lyrics, and ludicrous strokes of the brush all in the name of making a living and fulfilling a need to entertain the masses of human resources. Modern sculptures are welded parts of junk, modern paintings are meaningless splotches of colors, and modern music is discordant combinations of unnatural noise.

All these activities represent the soul fighting with itself. Industrialism offers no beauty for the soul, because beauty is a value that is experienced, not a process that is repeated. Frankly, the modern American does not know where to look for beauty. Nature has become dirty sidewalks, abandoned buildings, and rubble lots. Perhaps a mass-produced copy of a master adorns the dwelling with a shelf or two holding knickknacks made in China, but more than likely only photographs and posters cover the otherwise bare walls. Americans are unable to discern from the real and the sham, because beauty is considered a commodity to be bought, not an experience to be shared. Mass-produced trinkets, paintings, and music are pushed on consumers who mistake sentimentality for sentiment, confusion for simplicity, and vulgarity for dignity. For the most part, Americans are displaced foreigners who are merely consumers of overproduced goods and who refuse to produce anything cultural. In short, Americans, like their modern non-heroes, are takers, not givers.

It is too much to expect public educators to reverse this trend, since the soul of the student is not important. The student is trained to get as much out of life as possible. This expression may sound august, but young people naturally interpret this wisdom as one of taking, not giving. Not surprising then, whenever a school experiences a budget cut, the first courses to get the axe are art and music classes. Such courses are considered mostly for very gifted students who are out of touch with reality. Classes in art and music are perceived as offering nothing worthwhile for the student, because technical training instills in the student the desire to make money, not to contemplate about the beautiful. Nevertheless, schools do have active band programs, but the bands are merely utilitarian adjuncts for supporting the football team. Even then the music reflects generally the noise of the pop culture, which is no culture at all. The student who lusts for material goods will become too busy acquiring stuff to appreciate the beautiful. However, if they are successful and have a big enough bank account, then they figure that they can buy a *beautiful* house, a *beautiful* car, or any number of *beautiful* trinkets.

Nevertheless, the public schools are not the only culprits for the denigration of beauty in the United States. The ancient peoples could appreciate beauty, but often the beautiful was perverted and incorporated into the pagan mores and rites. On the other hand, the Hebrews understood where true beauty rested. Indeed, beauty is connected with worship, which centered on the beauty of *holiness*. What marked the Hebrews as being different from everyone else is summed up with one word: *simplicity*. In the beginning, their laws, their faith, and their conduct were models of simple living. Only when the scribes began to expand and to reinterpret the laws that governed their society did the Hebrews become encumbered with complexity. The law had lost its authority. When Jesus Christ appeared to restore the simplicity of the Hebrew law, the hearers were sincere when they declared that He spoke with authority and not like one of the scribes.

10. The Curriculum: Enriching the Soul with Art and Music

In like manner, simplicity marked the early church with its simplicity of worship and the simplicity of its gospel. Today, for the most part, the church is created in the image of Hollywood. The fraudulent glitz of thousands of modern churches across the land is a façade that hides assemblies of empty souls, desperately trying to entertain themselves in the name of Christianity. The hireling entertainers and psychologists, known by the worthy title of *pastor*, fail to offer anything of simplicity or beauty, because they have no authority by which to guide themselves or their congregations. These leaders are destined to rely upon their own subjectivity, being unable to offer any reasons why their subjectivity is superior to anyone else's assumptions. Instead of preserving that which is beautiful, the modern church champions the gaudy, the shallow, and the vulgar when choosing its architecture, its music, and its decorum. Indeed, it is truly written that the American church is "increased with goods, and have need of nothing" (Revelation 3:17), not even the simplicity of biblical faith.

Once again, the home school becomes important as a cultural institution. Every student should at least recognize beauty and appreciate art as an imitation of nature. The best way that a student can learn to appreciate beauty is by having a hobby. Just fifty years ago, most children had a hobby to fill the inevitable "nothing-to-do" segments of life. However, today's children do not engage themselves in hobbies, much to their detriment, like those of the past. With the roguish definition of leisure today, modern youths seek entertainment to occupy their lives. However, past generations of children had learned that a hobby was not entertainment that wasted life, but rather that it had a greater value. The young person truly becomes an expert in a field of knowledge. The origin of particular stamps or coins are discovered, the history of aviation is learned by the model aviator, or the scientific names and habits of *Lepidoptera* are memorized by the collector of butterflies. There is the sense of wonder as the young man applies the final decal to a scale model of *USS Constitution*.

For another example, while they do learn scientific knowledge about propulsion and trajectories, the model rocketeer, like any other modeler, is actually more interested in beauty. The young person careful applies several coats of sanding sealer to the fins, sanding between coats in order that the balsa wood will be like glass when painted. The prepping, the priming, and the final coats of paint are applied as if a great mural was being painted. The completed rocket is truly a work of art, a thing of beauty. The flight upward, and the descent of the rocket with its colorful, unfurled parachute being carried by the gentle breeze, is an experience of the soul that few will ever enjoy.

Also, the young girl who studies the markings of a rare stamp under the magnifying glass is truly in awe of the beauty of the lines, with their occasional flaws that produce their own unique beauty. Yet even stamp, coin, and doll collections have been cheapened by commercialism and industrialism, which overproduces "special edition collector items" for gullible consumers, who believe they are buying items of value. However, hobbies with their legitimate collections will always preserve that which can be rightfully called beautiful. Books, stamps, coins, and even memorabilia are collected primarily for the sake of the objects' beauty, not for a supposed investment. The collection as part of a hobby is surely a great service that students provide to their culture for the preservation of beauty.

In the home school, the student should be encouraged to participate in the arts in some form, which takes on many different

10. The Curriculum: Enriching the Soul with Art and Music

shapes. If the student is inclined toward writing, painting, drawing, or music, then these talents ought to be cultivated. Since the arts are disciplines that require special skills and knowledge, private lessons for students will be necessary if they are to fully explore their talents. Every student should try writing poetry. If anything is learned, the student will discover the value of words. Also, every student should try to learn to play a musical instrument. Nothing contributes more to the enrichment of neighbors than a young person who can play a piano or a classical guitar. While it is acknowledged that every student will not have a propensity toward writing poetry or the performing arts, every student should at least be given the opportunity to become acquainted with art and music. The flexibility of the home school allows for students to concentrate on their special talents without sacrificing the development of their heart, mind, and strength.

As already discussed in a previous chapter on leisure, the development of the soul was the prerogative of the privileged classes in past societies, and the true leisure class offered to their fellow countrymen the experiences of beauty. The art of the past endures because its simplicity speaks to all, its comprehension understood even by the dullest of souls. The beautiful is not appreciated today, because the soul is not appreciated. Since for the most part home educators do strive toward the perfecting of the souls of their students, from which emerges the beautiful, the home schools of America will most likely provide the next generation of artists, musicians, and writers, who will not only restore what is beautiful but will also breathe a living soul back into a dying way of life.

11 THE CURRICULUM
Enriching the Mind with Rhetoric

Ye know not what hurt ye do to learning, that care not for words but for matter, and so make a divorce betwixt the tongue and the heart.

—ROGER ASCHAM, *The Schoolmaster*

And he reasoned in the synagogue every sabbath, and persuaded the Jews and the Greeks.

—ACTS 18:4

The illiterates thronging American society have sullied—as they generally do to anything they touch—many perfectly fine words in the English language. One of these pitifully abused words is *rhetoric*. Whenever they disagree with anyone, the nitwits charge their opponent with the crime of "just using rhetoric." What do they expect their opponents to use? Gymnastics? Dullards are forever confusing rhetoric with sophistry. Even in his own day, Aristotle lacked patience with the writers of rhetoric, who emphasized trivialities.

In his book called (surprisingly enough) *Rhetoric*, Aristotle points out that rhetoricians favored writing about the subtle techniques used when speaking in court, because this kind of public speaking was easily corrupted by sophistry. While rhetoric is a noble exercise, speakers who use sophistry attempt to excite the emotions and the base passions of their hearers, particularly senators, jurors, and other mobs. However, according to Aristotle, a speaker uses rhetoric to champion truth by debating and defending, and to instruct others in truth; however, the speaker's audience must be hearers who are capable of choosing freely between alternatives. In short, sophistry uses emotional appeals, whereas rhetoric employs rational arguments. Therefore, the end of rhetoric is *persuasion* by honorable means, not by force or chicanery.

During the Middle Ages, rhetoric was neglected for the most part until the study of Roman law enjoyed a revival about AD 1100, when Irnerius taught law at the University of Bologna. But then the interest in rhetoric was not with speaking, but with writing. Medieval society had little need for public speaking, except for sermons. In addition to this, about the same time when Irnerius was teaching, Anselm began the scholastic school of learning. *Scholasticism* was the attempt to reconcile the teachings of the church with the ideas found in philosophy. The schoolmen tried to prove the validity of essential church doctrines through the use of human reason, relying upon logic. Such a task was a fool's errand, but the schoolmen tried nevertheless. By ignoring the Scriptures, Anselm offered his ontological argument for the existence of God. In other words, by analyzing the nature of God, one should be able to determine whether God is real or simply imagined. According to Anselm, if one can conceive of a great being with the attributes of God, then God must exist, because it is impossible to think of something that

11. The Curriculum: Enriching the Mind with Rhetoric

does not exist. In his *Proslogion*, Anselm asserts that God must exist because that "which nothing greater can be conceived, cannot exist in the understanding alone."

Of course, trying to prove something that cannot be proven leads to foolishness. Anyone can conceive of a being called a centaur. The image of a horse with the torso, the arms, and the head of a man is common in Greek mythology. Does it follow therefore that the centaur exists in the real world? Perhaps not, since no one has ever seen a centaur. But then again, perhaps yes. Just because no one has ever seen a centaur does not prove the nonexistence of the creature. Is it possible that centaurs existed before the great flood? Maybe. Thus, we begin to merrily chase our tails with our yes-no game. Indeed, creatures like centaurs and dinosaurs, or something of that ilk, might have existed at one time, because myths and legends are always based on some kernel of truth.

The problem rests upon the property called *existence*. One can imagine a cube as a solid object having six congruent square surfaces. This is both the nature and the definition of a cube. Furthermore, one can imagine the cube having different colors, sizes, and weights. Are these properties a part of the cube's nature or definition? No, because a cube is still a cube regardless of these qualities. Hence, is the existence of the cube essential to its nature? Again, the answer is no. A cube is a cube even if it does not exist. The following syllogism expresses Anselm's argument:

Premise: If I can conceive something in my mind, then it exists.
Premise: God can be conceived in my mind.
Therefore: God exists, *or*

$$\text{If } P \text{ then } Q$$
$$P$$
$$\text{Therefore } Q$$

No one can disagree with the reasoning here. However, while the argument is valid, the conclusion may be true or false depending to the truth of the premises. As discussed above, Q is not always true, and thus no one is obligated to accept the argument. Fortunately for humankind, God does not have to rely on human reason for His existence.

Herein is the weakness of basing a system of education solely on logic. Whether the statements in the argument are true or false are of no concern to logic. Anselm's scholasticism relied upon the syllogism, which was fatal. While pure education and scholasticism do not claim to discover any new knowledge, pure education is an onward clarification of the best in one's culture, whereas scholasticism with its deductive logic fails to clarify anything. The syllogism can only determine whether an argument has validity, not whether the conclusion of an argument is right or wrong. Scholasticism was given an impossible task to accomplish.

As pointed out before, Eastern thought and Western thought are incompatible and cannot be reconciled, making an impossible marriage of the two. Not only did it fail as an internal project, but scholasticism was being challenged by external forces also. The momentum toward experimentation and observation of nature began to take precedence over lecture halls. With laboratories indoors and out, science along with induction was overtaking scholasticism, not rapidly, but steadily in the quest for knowledge. As a serious discipline, rhetoric would have to remain dormant until the Renaissance.

During the Renaissance, rhetoric became associated at first with manners. In his *Book of the Courtier*, Castiglione explained that the gentleman was to conduct himself with such grace that if

11. The Curriculum: Enriching the Mind with Rhetoric

he were defeated in an endeavor, he would not be embarrassed by his failure. On the other hand, if the gentleman were successful in any enterprise that he undertook, then he should expect a lot of praise for his accomplishment. Not only was his outward conduct important, but the way that the gentleman wrote and spoke was important as well. According to Castiglione, rhetoric was a tool to be used to climb the ladder of success within the court. Indeed, the goal was to get others to praise the gentleman without his bragging on himself.

> ... *[T]o my thinking, the whole art consists in saying things in such a way that they shall not seem to be said to that end, but let fall so naturally that it was impossible not to say them, and while seeming always to avoid self-praise, yet to achieve it; but not after the manner of those boasters, who open their mouths and let the words come forth haphazard.*

To be plainly stated, rhetoric was to be ironic and deceptive. Fortunately, rhetoric was not destined to become simply the tool of sycophants, because some of the schools revived the rhetorical ideas of Cicero and Quintilian. According to these Roman orators, rhetoric has a didactic purpose, a purpose that teaches and educates. In *Institutio Oratoria*, his famous work on rhetoric, Quintilian outlines the course of study for the statesman, who ought to be both philosopher and orator. First of all, students of rhetoric should read incessantly. This reading will help students toward being moral persons in the sense that they can discern between right and wrong. This is important because public speaking "is in the main concerned with the treatment of what is just and honorable." In other words, the speaker's motive is to guide men to right actions.

Also, according to Quintilian, the message must come from the heart and be delivered with enthusiasm. Therefore, speakers must believe their messages. Because this is true, the speaker is motivated by what is good for friends, neighbors, and country, and not by greed and ambition. But this does not mean that the orator will treat lightly the arguments of opponents. In fact, orators will understand the arguments of their opponents so well that they should have compelling rebuttals and should be able to present the arguments as if they were their own.

If the role of public speakers is to guide their audience to right actions, then they should study what is the difference between that which is righteous and that which is unrighteous. The reason for learning the difference is so that good will ultimately prevail. According to the Roman way of thinking, what represents good was anything that fulfilled a duty first to the family, and then to country. Therefore, central to Quintilian's rhetoric is the concept of "the good man," and not the charlatan of Castiglione's deceit.

Whether students are speaking or writing, their rhetoric should be motivated by honesty. But in addition to this, students should strive for clarity of expression. Both Cicero and Quintilian agree writing is a necessary skill for success as an orator. Many of the Roman orators would write their speeches first before memorizing them. The orator would deliver his speech so naturally that few would realize how much work went into the preparation of the speech. Charles Spurgeon was in the habit of writing his sermons completely in manuscript form, of memorizing the words, and then of delivering the message just as he had prepared it. Again, in his *Institutio Oratoria*, Quintilian states, "It is in writing that the eloquence has its roots and foundations, it is writing that provides the

11. The Curriculum: Enriching the Mind with Rhetoric

treasure house where the wealth of oratory is stored, and whence it is produced to meet the demands of sudden emergencies." Even Cicero would agree with Quintilian that the best statesman-orator will be the one who can both speak and write equally well.

Therefore, an essential part of pure education is the use of rhetoric in both composition and speaking. In his *Summing Up*, W. Somerset Maugham declares that a reader should never have to exert any effort to know what the writer is saying. Indeed, the mark of good writers are those who can clearly express their ideas without severely taxing their readers' cognitive abilities. But the reason why most students fail to write well is revealed by Sinclair Lewis, "Writing is just work—there's no secret. If you dictate or use a pen or type or write with your toes—it is still just work." Yes, writing requires effort, and unfortunately, things that require effort are postponed for a more convenient day, which never comes. The key to writing well is practice, practice, and more practice. While being led to write, in the end, students alone must determine that they will compose—anything.

But here is the dilemma. In order to write well, the student must practice writing. Okay, but most students would rather have a beating instead of writing even one paragraph. Like the student who does not know but only reads, this reluctance to write arises from the student's having no ideas to write about. For a writing program, Quintilian's system is rivaled by few. At the earliest possible age, the student should engage in grammar studies, which center on *what* the student should know. According to Quintilian, not only does grammar allow the student to imitate the best in writing and speaking, but also the student learns to interpret poetry. In order to do this, the student must be resigned to reading.

As for writing, students at first copy passages from the great poets, orators, and writers, and then at a later stage of their education they paraphrase the passages into their own words. At first, students imitate other writers' styles, and later their own unique style emerges as they write their own fables and short poems, which are supplemented with written essays about morality.

While grammar focuses on the *what* of education, rhetoric centers on the *how*, which is the application of grammar. Most elementary schools do a tolerable business with preparing students to read and write. On the other hand, the middle and secondary schools fail miserably, because grammar is still the focus, whether in English, foreign language, or history classes. Of course, most educators believe that the study of rhetorical writing is neither required nor important for technical training and for getting a job. But the students are the poorer for their schools' neglect. Rhetoric exists as a human endeavor, which explores not only the human predicament, but human desires as well. Writing about the great issues of life helps students to become more aware of themselves. C. Day Lewis is correct when he states that writers write to understand, not to be understood. Nothing stretches the young person's heart and mind better than writing.

Also, writing helps the student to become aware of the human experience at large. Since these experiences are different among various groups of people, rhetoric tends to be culturally bound. Interestingly, even concerning the belles lettres, the best of American literature is *regional* in setting and ideas. Indeed, Kenneth Burke suggests that the *primary* role of modern rhetoric is not persuasion but *identification*. Even though all writers or speakers should consciously identify with their audience, Burke goes even further

11. The Curriculum: Enriching the Mind with Rhetoric

by allowing an unconscious desire in the individual to belong in an association of like-minded people.

While greatly benefiting from their understanding the regional idiosyncrasies of others, students should choose expressing all thoughts cogently and concisely if they have to choose between either belonging or clarity. Regarding clarity, Quintilian would have the student learn more about advanced principles in rhetoric, which center on the classical form for argument. The form has a beginning, a body, and a conclusion, applicable to both writing and speaking. However, the practice of rhetorical writing must be started as soon as possible after the grammar stage of a student's education. According to the educational literature on writing, a student will require three years of constant practice in order to become proficient with this form of writing. However, by writing papers *and* speeches, the student should cut this time in half.

While rhetorical writing is neglected in the schools, rhetorical speaking is ignored just as badly; indeed, worse. If a course in speech is offered at a secondary school, the class is an elective usually for one semester only. As with writing, the student cannot become proficient in public speaking by memorizing a few declamations or preparing a pantomime for the entertainment of classmates. However, memorization of declamations and poetry does belong in the grammar stage of the student's education. The student should feel the words, and in order to feel the words, the student must *know* the meaning of the words. The educator should quiz the student on every word in the selection, and the student should offer a satisfactory definition for every word. Nothing is more pitiful than watching a student recite Shakespeare's "Sonnet 116" without emotion, and worst, without knowledge.

However, students should come to the point when they set aside childish memorization and begin to contemplate rhetorical issues in any passage from a speech or a poem. No longer do students copy or memorize the words of others, but they use their own words to enlarge or to criticize the ideas contained in the words. With any rhetorical issue, the student should write or speak about the subject intelligently and passionately. But all is in vain if students fail to have a ready supply of ideas with which to employ and to aid them.

Therefore, at the risk of sounding redundant, the student must be encouraged to read from the best among books and poetry. Early in the grammar studies, the student should learn writing by first copying passages from the Authorized Version of the English Bible as well as from other literature. Reciting portions of speeches, poetry, and Bible verses along with learning the rules of language should be the mainstay of the grammar education. This is true with the foreign and ancient languages as well. After copying from the masters for a short time, students should begin writing their own creative works, as opposed to critical ones, which touch essentially the soul, not the mind. These writings would include short stories and poems. Yet the student should be careful to employ correct principles of grammar while writing.

Sometime during the middle school years, the student should begin rhetorical studies. Writing and speaking will center on critical analysis and not creative writing. Later in their schooling, students may wish to read books about rhetoric, particularly those of Aristotle, Cicero, and Quintilian. At first, the student should practice writing by organizing thoughts with the in-class essay using the simple seven-sentence format for about a year before composing

11. The Curriculum: Enriching the Mind with Rhetoric

any argumentative paper with its five-paragraph format. Students should begin employing rhetoric in public life as soon as possible. To give some incentive to write well, have the student write articles for magazines, newsletters, or newspapers, especially letters to the editor. By seeing their words published and their name in print, students will be motivated to improve their skills.

The delivery of speeches should be frequent, both prepared and impromptu. If several home schools are within a nearby area, families should encourage their students to debate with one another and even form literary societies, which should be an extension of the English cooperatives. Also, literary societies ought to be formed for foreign and ancient languages as well. The effort will be well worth the time, even if only two or three schools participate. The more opportunities students have to write and to speak, the more proficient they will become by helping to lead their readers and hearers from darkness into light.

With their writing and speaking in three separate languages, when will the student ever find time to study for tests in literature, rhetoric, and the other disciplines? First of all, the only legitimate examination is students' daily application of loving their neighbors. However, tests are unfortunately part of the educational baggage, and the home school has no choice but to tote the unwieldy things. The plain truth of the matter is that the disciplines that affect the heart and soul cannot be tested, because nothing is really learned; the learning is experienced. Divergent knowledge is open-ended without right or wrong answers. If a test must be given, then do not use any objective tests, which use true-false, matching, and multiple-choice questions. If literature or rhetoric is presented as thousands of pieces of data to be processed, then the student stays on a level plain, never advancing upward. Ideally, students should be examined orally and thereby have to defend their positions to the educator, or in the alternative, they should be required to write essays on rhetorical issues. Pure education is about principles and the application of those principles. Therefore, is it not absolutely necessary for the student to be tested on content. The best examination is to have the student speak or write extemporaneously. The educator should examine the student for expression of ideas that are uniquely the student's work and for presentation of cogent thinking. Also, this criterion applies to papers and speeches, which ought to be evaluated as well.

It is hoped that what students will eventually come to realize regarding pure education is that the great writers and poets of the past do not desire to pass on mere intelligence but rather enjoyment and delight, which cannot be learned but must be experienced. Knowledge keeps the student near the earth; delight takes the student heavenward. However, to truly benefit the student, this delight needs to be shared with others. Therefore, the educator must avoid giving the student the impression that education is simply preparing for tests and giving a correct answer.

Noise and hurry are the incessant enemies of the student's peace of mind. The one makes deep thinking and contemplation impossible, and the other steals the time meant for leisure. In mass-produced training, the student as machine seldom struggles with finding the right word to express the right idea. Nor are ideas seen as opposites—as light and darkness, as truth and error. Ideas are seen as unconnected. Viewing ideas as separate, unrelated entities may explain the madness of the abortionist, who is appalled by the death penalty for capital offenses. While claiming to oppose

11. The Curriculum: Enriching the Mind with Rhetoric

capital punishment, the abortionist supports the death penalty for innocents, whose only misfortune was to be conceived in America. Yet the poor dullard believes that the child is only potential life and that this belief makes abortion acceptable. But what kind of potential life is involved here? A cow? The one thing needful to keep the cobwebs out of the brain is good, old-fashioned rhetoric. No reading, no writing, and no thinking will lead to slavery, both physically and spiritually. Upon the anvil of apathy, the hammer of tyranny is relentlessly forging manacles with tempered ignorance. Students who read and write well, who defend their positions passionately and reasonably, and who know their opponents thoroughly will forever be a free people.

12 THE CURRICULUM
Enriching the Mind with Moral Philosophy

This is no case of petty right or wrong
That politicians or philosophers
Can judge. I hate not Germans, nor grow hot
With love of Englishmen, to please newspapers.

—Edward Thomas, *"This Is No Case of Petty Right or Wrong"*

For they know not to do right, saith the LORD, who store up violence and robbery in their palaces.

—Amos 3:10

While most of his verse focused on rural life in England, Edward Thomas wrote a few poems about the war in Europe. Enlisting in 1915, Thomas had his literary career cut short when he was killed in action in 1917. With the creation of the nation-state, war has become extremely terrifying. The first modern war between nation-states occurred in North America between the United States and the Confederate States of America. The casualties were shockingly high. The military leaders for both countries were schooled in the tactics of the European mode of warfare; but modern weapons made the tactics obsolete, even though the dying was quite up-to-date. Ironclad ships, submarines with torpedoes, observation balloons, improved cannons, improved rifles, railway transportation, telegraph messages, prisoner-of-war camps, and conscription of citizens were the innovations that were used in the War between the States. But the greatest innovation of all was the use of psychological warfare, waged by General William T. Sherman against the defenseless civilians of Georgia, South Carolina, and North Carolina. Civilian targets were now valid objectives, and the means were centered on terrorism. Since the time the Confederate States were forced to rejoin the American Empire, wars have become more brutal and more terrifying. No doubt, the next world war will be a splendid affair.

The creation of the nation-state is partially responsible for the rivers of blood. Yet since the nineteenth century, most of the nation-states have historically been representative democracies. Why would citizens wish for the best of their youth to be hazarded on a battlefield to be killed or maimed? Alas, the question of war is never given to the citizens for a vote. Indeed, common people do not start wars; governments do. One can understand the necessity of protecting the nation from an unprovoked attack, but it is more difficult to understand the motives behind the politicians' wanting to commit citizens to a conflict that does not threaten the welfare of the nation directly. One must conclude that war must be profitable for someone. If any political decision violates common sense, one should follow the money trail to see who will profit by the insane decision.

12. The Curriculum: Enriching the Mind with Moral Philosophy

About the same time when the nation-states were being created, the industrial revolution also was getting started. At first, factories tended to be local, serving a region rather than seeking markets in an entire country. However, during the twentieth century, along with mass-production came the need to sale the overproduction, which is the inevitable result of industrialism. Not too much intelligence is required to realize that the competition for national and international markets will mean conflict eventually. Politicians provide the cause, industry provides the guns, and citizens provide the blood. John Dewey suggested that war could be eliminated after the world becomes one happy community. Then by fiat, this world democracy would merely outlaw war, like any other crime. A more practical solution to ending warfare is to require all corporate board members and officers along with all national politicians, regardless of age, to be the first to be drafted into the armed forces, whereby they can demonstrate their leadership and patriotism. This plan will surely end most warfare.

But what does this initial discussion about warfare have to do with moral philosophy? At the heart of war is the idea of obligations and duties. For individual citizens, the call to arms poses some profound questions concerning beliefs about right and wrong and relationships to the government. The struggle with questions about right actions and just government is the subject matter of moral philosophy, which is further divided into ethics and politics. The division between Hebrew and Greek thinking cannot be sharper than when concerning moral philosophy. Basically, the Hebrew notion of obeying revealed law leads the citizen to live a peaceable life, whenever possible, with all men. Man's obligations are clearly revealed, and there is no need for outside interference. Citizens do right because they will give an account of themselves eventually to God, not to man. Indeed, if the moral choice is between obeying God or man, the citizen should unhesitatingly obey the ultimate judge of all men. Therefore, it follows that the particular form of government under which individuals find themselves is of no consequence. One can obey God under a democracy or a dictatorship— as is true around the world today.

On the other hand, Western moral philosophy is divided into three camps. First, Plato and Aristotle believed that morality and the just state center on happiness. The happy citizen is by far the moral citizen. But Plato also believed that the moral citizen is a reasonable one as well. If a society has a criminal class, then it is because of the ignorance of the poor, benighted crooks who failed to learn that crime does not pay. Thus the role of the state is simply to force (in a paternal sort of way, of course) citizens into developing good habits that will bring happiness.

Second, also thinking happiness to be an end, John Stuart Mill posits his utility principle. The core of utilitarian thinking can be summed up as "actions are right in proportion as they tend to promote happiness, wrong as they tend to produce the reverse of happiness." Mill expands this idea by democratizing it to mean the *greatest happiness for the greatest number of citizens*. While Plato envisioned a paternalistic philosopher-king providing guidance for his happy subjects, Mill daydreams that the majority of happy winners and the minority of less-than-happy losers can coexist in a harmonious society, where both will promote the general welfare. The problem with philosopher-kings and majorities is that they want to preserve their self-interest and to keep their tenacious grip on the power that they have. Whenever the power elite can get away

12. The Curriculum: Enriching the Mind with Moral Philosophy

with it, they will create problems in order to grab more power. The best way to accomplish this power-grabbing is by declaring war, whether on Germany, Vietnam, poverty, drugs, illiteracy, or hate. While the Greeks thought one leader was enough for determining fair and foul, Mill gives this august role to the mob.

Finally, reasonable citizens would view these two moral theories based on happiness to be deficient, unless they should be the dictator or one of the politicians leading the happy gang that currently is in power. Immanuel Kant also disagreed with the theories. According to Kant, morality exists not in the consequences (that is, promoting happiness), but in the rightness of the motive. Therefore, right actions are determined whenever an individual can universalize the particular action. For example, if a boy wishes to steal a candy bar from a store, then he should honestly state as a maxim, "Stealing is an honorable thing to do." Since the boy is unable to accept this maxim, because his possessions, including his person, are at risk, then stealing is an immoral action. This *categorical imperative*, as Kant calls it, is unconditional. In other words, it is never right to steal, and most people would agree that stealing is wrong, even if the thief is hungry.

The trouble is not when citizens analyze one moral principle at a time. Conflict occurs when several duties are colliding. For example, all citizens have the duty to obey the law of the land. Also, individuals ought to love their neighbors according to a higher law. If the law of the land became such that all books were to be brought to central locations for burning, what should citizens do if a friend gives them some books and asks for them to be hidden? Should they obey the law? Should they refuse their friend's request? Should they report their friend to the authorities? Should they take their friend's books, but then take the books for burning? So on and so forth. In other words, right actions are seldom—if ever—easy ones. If citizens find themselves in such dilemmas, the reason is because the civil authorities think they know better how to direct the lives of citizens.

Therefore, regarding moral philosophy, the Western tradition stresses an activist role for both defining and enforcing that which is determined to be right. The laws of the United States are never fixed, because progress is never static. A legislative session is considered a failure "if something isn't done." It is this *something* that causes thinking people some concern, because eventually the vast number of somethings will conflict with one another. Frankly, most Americans would be very willing for their representatives to collect their salaries by just sitting at their desks *and by doing nothing*. But the do-gooders believe that they have got to do something. However, the more laws that a legislature imposes upon its citizens, the more enslaved the people will become. Indeed, the more complex and the more numerous the laws of a nation, the more primitive the society becomes.

By contrast, the Hebrew tradition emphasizes a passive role, because the law is revealed. All that is required of the people and their government is to obey. The laws of the Hebrews were not complex, but neither were their laws derived from human reason. Laws against covetousness suggest divine origin, because human judges cannot discern covetousness. This moral wrong is committed with the heart, which only God can judge. The laws against sodomy, incest, and bestiality marked the Hebrews as unique, since these practices were common in the lands surrounding Israel. From a moral point of view, if sodomy is acceptable behavior, then incest

12. The Curriculum: Enriching the Mind with Moral Philosophy

and bestiality must also be accepted. However, if incest and bestiality are revolting to one's sensibilities, then this disgust is in line with the revealed law, not anything derived from human reason. Only in the revealed law is all sexual deviancy unacceptable; human reason is unable to condemn the behavior. Because they were for the most part a responsible people, the Hebrews were free to practice their laws and way of life under many different governments, some even occupational regimes. While it is true that they were often misunderstood and mistreated, the Hebrews developed their own unique culture, which remains today. Clearly, the Hebrew tradition and history reveal that the Jewish people were a people who desired to mind their own business and seldom imposed their will upon others.

In short, the Western tradition produces busybodies who think they know what is best morally for everyone else, and the Hebrew tradition produces responsible citizens who wish to be left alone. Therefore it is not surprising to find the United States divided into two major camps. The Northern and Pacific Coast sections try to force their self-righteous ideas on the Southern and Western sections, who wish the do-gooders would just mind their own business. The reason for this division between regions is that the folks in the South and West value an agrarian tradition, which includes a respect for a Godly morality, a weak government at all levels, and a citizen's self-reliance. On the other hand, the North and Pacific Coast, with their love for progress, insist on an overreaching national government that protects victim-classes from state and county governments, a coerced acceptance of immoral behavior, and a citizen's dependence on a socialistic government. Of course, each section will have those of both camps within its borders, like

Atlanta is a center of progressivism within Georgia, but the predominate tradition of the state remains agrarian. Between the two worldviews, there can be no compromise.

Regarding American political parties, many citizens have become dismayed by the apparent lack of choices between candidates, particularly with national elections. The reason for this chagrin is easy: the United States has no opposition party. From the beginning, American politics has been centered on *compromise,* and the worst tag a politician can get attached to him, besides being called a racist, is being a *partisan*. The U.S. Constitution is a document of compromise. The legislative history before the War between the States was one of continuous compromise. When the Southerners could no longer compromise with the North, the Confederates left the Union *peaceable* and wanted to be left alone. This was unacceptable for the *sectional,* Republican do-gooders. Today, the losing political gang yells and screams for a spirit of bipartisanship. With over two hundred years of compromising (except for a brief four-year period during which differences of opinion were worth dying for), no one should wonder why there fails to be a difference between the two major parties.

Both national parties see human salvation through power politics, both parties embrace the Western tradition and scorn the Eastern one (unless the candidate can win some votes with support of traditional family values), and both parties have a history of troubling peaceful citizens who are content to be left alone. From the discussion above, the Western and the Eastern traditions have no common ground for compromise—period. Since neither major party is in sympathy with the Eastern tradition, then well over 50 percent of Americans, who value the ideals of agrarianism, self-re-

12. The Curriculum: Enriching the Mind with Moral Philosophy

liance, and revealed morality, are not represented in the national Congress at all. What is needed is an opposition party that will oppose the Western tradition of moral philosophy.

But this lack of representation is also true to some extent in many state and local governments as well. Currently, state and local politics should be the focus of home educators' energy. By being distracted by the big national picture, citizens can lose sight of their own backyards. However bleak the political outlook presents itself, the home educator should adopt her school's moral philosophy from the Hebrew tradition. First of all, this tradition has an infallible guide for determining right actions. The student need not struggle to discover the principles of morality; the principles are already revealed. For the student, the action required is not one of discovery, but one of obedience.

But second, the Hebrew tradition mirrors what home educators are trying to accomplish. By seceding from the public school system, home educators are announcing to the government that they wish to be left alone in order to teach their students to become responsible, self-reliant citizens, and not shallow-thinking workers dependent upon the industrial-governmental cartel. The home educator should remember the goal of pure education, which is to direct the self-governing student to love God and neighbors. The home-educated student may be an elitist who enjoys the privileged status of being *educated*, but the student is checked by the Scriptures from becoming self-righteous.

However, even though the home school should immerse itself in the Hebrew tradition, the student should study the moral philosophies found in the Western tradition. This study is not for students to pick the theories that strike them as plausible. The theories of

Plato, Aristotle, Mill, and Kant are all flawed. The endless wrangling between the individual and the collective as stated in the theories of libertarianism and egalitarianism will only guarantee that the students will be running in circles. The tension in government has always been the balance between the individual and the mob. The purpose of this study is not for students to choose the least of many evils, but rather to know their enemies with their machination.

Regarding the formation of the governmental systems at the national and state levels, the United States is assuredly the product of the Western tradition, and more specifically, of the Enlightenment. However, the Hebrew concepts of the rights of all human beings with the ideas of equality, liberty, and property have been reinterpreted by human reason. Likewise, the notions of fairness and justice are badly mangled today. Since the battle in politics is often one of emotion against logic, the student should be able to recognize the origin of such arguments. If the abortionist claims a legal right to butcher children, then the student should be aware that the actual principle is one of happiness: the abortionist is happy with collecting fees, and the mother is happy to get rid of her *unhappiness*. The student then can intelligently attack the immoral act as philosophically and morally unacceptable, and any law that allows abortion is just plain nonsense, and ought to be reversed immediately in states that still permit it. The home educator is educating leaders, and leaders need to know how their enemies think and what their motives are.

For the student, reading from Plato's *Republic* and Aristotle's *Politics* will be of some usefulness. Machiavelli's *Prince* is a must. The works by Kant are frankly unreadable, even in German, and Mill takes plenty of unpacking. The political works by Hobbes,

12. The Curriculum: Enriching the Mind with Moral Philosophy

Locke, and Rousseau are difficult to read, but will be profitable, if read slowly and carefully. Nietzsche is not for the faint of heart (or mind). Actually, if students read Jack London's *Call of the Wild* and *White Fang*, then they will know everything they need to know about Nietzsche's superman. Students who are interested in uniquely American theory of politics should not overlook the writings of John Adams, John C. Calhoun, or Alexander Stephens. Also, closely connected with the theory of ethics and politics is the study of economics. *The Wealth of Nations* by Adam Smith is a must for understanding capitalism. The works of Adolph Hitler and Karl Marx have fairly good translations; however, the works are lengthy. Hundreds of other books exist that comment on these major works. A reading of the Declaration of Independence and the U.S. Constitution with their history will put the student among the few that have ever read these documents, much less how they became a byword in the land of the semi-free.

The above books should be read by students during their years of secondary education. Before this time, however, the student should read several of the many introductions to ethics and politics. Reading, not testing, should be emphasized with ethics and politics. Little purpose can be served by having the student tested on what was read. However, the student should be encouraged to find ethical and political ideas that are used by current individuals, both conservative and liberal, and to determine the correctness in their thinking. To determine whether the politician is using ideas from Western or Eastern thinking will be most valuable. In addition to this, the exercise will prove greatly entertaining.

Also, one final consideration is in order here. Those who follow the Hebrew tradition of minding their own business usually become disturbed whenever they have to actively participate and "take to the streets." The radical activism of the self-righteous busybodies has forced quiet, peaceable people to do much more than just cast their ballots once every two years for the lesser of two evils. The home schools should be leading the way toward neutralizing, if not defeating, the *immoral* agenda of the elitists. The home schools with their students should become involved with the many organizations that help preserve regional heritage, support home education, and minimize centralization. If the parents own a business, then they should prayerfully consider joining a local civic organization. Many home educators should become active participants in local political organizations, and students will get a better understanding of the machinery of political action by being a part of the process. If there is a bent toward maybe participating later in politics, these students would do well to join a political club; in fact, the earlier the better.

 Maybe by getting more home-educated leaders in the positions of authority, the next generation will not need to fight as much as today's responsible citizens must. Unfortunately, we can no longer rest easy in Zion, since the Greeks are no longer hiding in their wooden horse.

13 THE CURRICULUM
Enriching the Mind with Mathematics

But arithmetic, geometry, and other such disciplines—which treat of nothing but the simplest and most general things and which are indifferent as to whether these things do or do not exist—contain something certain and indubitable.

....
—RENÉ DESCARTES, *Meditations on First Philosophy*

Behold, this have I found, saith the preacher, counting one by one, to find out the account.

....
—ECCLESIASTES 7:27

In the year 799, Pope Leo III was attacked in the streets of Rome. The mistreated vicar of Christ fled like a tormented cur across the Alps and sought the protection of Charles the Great. Charles happened to like Leo, so he went to Rome and roughed up Leo's persecutors. On Christmas Day, year 800, while Charles was hearing mass in the church of Saint Peter, the restored Pope Leo placed a crown upon his protector's head and proclaimed Charlemagne to be emperor and Augustus. Whether Leo had authority to crown anyone did not seem to bother the church attendees, because the folks applauded and cheered wildly with enthusiasm. Undoubtedly, his good fortune was justified, for Charlemagne was truly a great ruler. Part of his greatness centers on his being an educated man, who studied rhetoric, logic, arithmetic, and astronomy. In addition to this, Charlemagne encouraged learning among his children and his subjects. The unsung hero for the revival of learning called the "Carolingian Renaissance" was an English theologian named Alcuin. It was Alcuin of York who is credited with reestablishing, if not actually creating, the curriculum of the seven liberal arts, which were divided into the Trivium and the Quadrivium. Alcuin used the liberal arts as the basis for an elementary education. However, later during the Middle Ages, the focus was shifted to learning Latin at the elementary level and to studying the Trivium and Quadrivium at the university.

While the home school community has made much about the Trivium, which consists of grammar, logic, and rhetoric, the other four liberal arts comprising the Quadrivium have not been nearly as noised about in the various journals, newsletters, or blogs. The Quadrivium includes the four mathematical studies of arithmetic, geometry, astronomy, and music. In the medieval universities, the Trivium was the course of study for the undergraduates. Only after students began graduate studies were they introduced to the Quadrivium. Yet modern school boards have insisted that the college-bound student must have four years of mathematics, while neglecting rhetoric completely, which is the one discipline the college-bound student needs above all other preparatory courses.

13. The Curriculum: Enriching the Mind with Mathematics

Board members, superintendents, and educators really do have a "fair is foul" mentality when majoring on the minors. One wonders why this should be so. Many college programs require very little, if any, mathematics and science, particularly with humanities and pre-law degrees.

In reality, mathematics just was not that important during the Middle Ages. Only in the thirteenth century, with the introduction of Arabic numerals, which included the zero, did arithmetic begin to flourish as a useful tool for commerce and money-making, but not as a theoretical pursuit. As for geometry, the Romans used its principles primarily for surveying, and this knowledge was discarded later. However, when Abelard of Bath translated Euclid's *Elements of Geometry* into Latin in the year 1120, students took a new interest in geometry.

As for astronomy, most prior knowledge of the cosmos was lost until the thirteenth century, when the secrets of this science were rediscovered from the Muslims during the Crusades. The first book introduced in Europe was the *Almagest* by Claudius Ptolemeus, or Ptolemy, with the Islamic commentaries concerning his theories. With these materials, astronomy became the most popular subject among students. Regarding music, today most students would doubt that the study of music is a course in mathematics, unless they take a class in music theory. Then all doubt will be removed. During the Middle Ages, the discipline of music was not for the bettering of the performing arts but was studied as a mathematical and theoretical subject.

The one admirable quality about mathematics is its predictability. According to Descartes, mathematics has correct answers, both "certain and indubitable." Since this is true, then mathematics belongs to convergent knowledge where there are right and wrong answers. Students seem to take comfort in knowing that something in life has answers. What most students despise about mathematics is the processes that they must memorize and use in order to get the right answers. But now enters the calculator. Fortunately, the Western world rejected the Greek and Roman symbols and adopted the Arabic numerals for its numbers. The elegant but confusing Greek χξϛ and the bold but clumsy Roman DCLXVI cannot prevail against the simplicity of the Arabic 666. The fact that the Arabic numerals are positional offers a great advantage over the Greek and Latin, because each symbol, depending on its position, represents a different value. But in addition to this, Simon Stevin, a Belgium engineer, posited the theory of decimal numbers, a theory that was not well accepted in Europe until the seventeenth century. With positional symbols and decimals, the calculator was made possible, because solving for any x is merely a process. Anything that is a process can be reduced to a mechanical function, and thus the human mind as well as human labor can be bypassed.

But in that it is *both* mentally manipulated and physically applied, mathematics thereby acquires its uniqueness. Oddly, mathematical concepts such as lines and points, which theoretically have no dimensions, are violated the moment a line is drawn or a point is indicated on a piece of paper. The student can never draw a perfect square to prove that the sum of its four angles equals 360 degrees. In the physical world, proof becomes impossible. Through mathematical proofs, the student can easily do so, but only in the realm of intellect. Thus, mathematics provides a precarious bridge between the physical and metaphysical worlds. The discipline joins the intellect and the senses together, because while they can be

13. The Curriculum: Enriching the Mind with Mathematics

represented physically, mathematical concepts are perfect only as an ideal. In his great chain of being, Plato understood this relationship as a line that separated *thinking* from *belief* and mathematical objects from visible objects. Indeed, both Plato and Descartes believed that a thorough study of mathematics was necessary before any serious concentration in philosophy could take place. Mathematics helps the would-be philosopher to transcend the physical world into the mental expanse.

No one doubts nor denies the usefulness of mathematics in technology and the sciences. But with the exception of arithmetic, without which, according to Benjamin Franklin, business could not manage, mathematics still has little to do with providing wisdom for human life. Regardless of our Age of Technology, even arithmetic is valuable in life only to ensure that a shopper is not being shortchanged by the scanner when checking out purchases. While drawing their Cartesian-coordinate graphs and plotting their ordered pairs, students instinctively ask, "What good is this stuff?" Of course, math teachers use the perennial answer that seems to pacify the grumbling from the insurrectionary scholars, "Because educated people are supposed to know this stuff." The students may tolerate this maxim, but they are never convinced of its sagacity.

Later on, just as they suspected, millions of graduates from high school and college discover that their knowledge of set theory or of the Pythagorean theorem is seldom, if ever, applied in the real world. Even mathematicians are hard pressed to find reasons for teaching their craft to non-mathematicians, who are quite contented to remain mathematically-challenged. To make mathematics "useful" to the vast majority—who could not care less—college survey courses in mathematics include chapters about probability, statistics, and matrix theories. As for the usefulness of these disciplines, one can learn the value of slot machines, the skewing of figures to suit oneself, and in the context of game theory, a strategy against an opponent in order to keep one's money while bilking the worthy opponent (who failed to study game theory) of his. Useful indeed!

This perceived uselessness of mathematics centers on what the subject brings to everyday living—*nothing*. Quadratic equations, Venn diagrams, and irrational numbers add nothing, explain nothing, and expand nothing in life. But this is the nature of the beast. Mathematics does not clarify anything, because it is the needless repetition of ideas by using different symbols. In logic, this redundancy is called a *tautology*, or $p = p$. In life, this is called just plain silliness. For example, *Jim is just being Jim*. Another form of tautology is $p \vee \sim p$, *Either it's raining, or it's not raining*. The statement is so obvious that no one can argue about its truthfulness. In like manner, when $5 + 2 = 7$, what new ideas are revealed in *5* and *2* or *7*? Regardless how complicated the equation may become, such as

$$4y = 5(x - 2)^2 - 8$$

the result provides nothing new by which wisdom is gained. In short, mathematics is the study of tautologies. When a student sees a fellow student (who happens to be a close friend) cheating on an examination, the student's knowledge that there is a subset of cheaters in the larger set of all students will not provide wisdom about how to deal with the friend's cheating.

Even Descartes became bewildered by the inability of mathematics to exercise a greater role in human life. In his *Discourse on Method*, Descartes attempts to create a basis for knowledge that

13. The Curriculum: Enriching the Mind with Mathematics

would be as certain as the disciplines in mathematics. His method was to reject everything that he believed to be true through his senses, which could deceive him, and seek only ideas that were "clear and distinct," in other words, self-evident truths. At first, Descartes considers mathematics as a basis for his method, but after some reflection, he rejects it.

I took especially great pleasure in mathematics because of the certainty and the evidence of its arguments. But I did not yet notice its true usefulness and, thinking that it seemed useful only to the mechanical arts, I was astonished that, because its foundations were so solid and firm, no one had built anything more noble upon them.

Descartes apparently thinks "the mechanical arts" are less noble than the issues of life, which he feels needed to be cataloged scientifically. Geometry and algebra were included with the mathematics that Descartes studied while growing up. After criticizing the two disciplines, Descartes concludes that both fall short of usefulness for enriching the student:

. . . as to the analysis of the ancients and the algebra of the moderns, apart from the fact that they apply only to very abstract matters and seem to have no practical utility, the former is always so subject to the consideration of figures that it cannot exercise the understanding without exhausting the imagination; and in the case of algebra, one is so governed by certain laws and symbols that out of it has been made a confused and obscure art that encumbers the mind instead of a science that cultivates it.

If a mathematician like Descartes suggests that geometry "[exhausts] the imagination," and that algebra "encumbers the mind" rather than cultivating it, then why is there such an emphasis on mathematics in the schools and in the curriculum? Surely there is a better reason than "Well, educated people are supposed to know this stuff."

Perhaps mathematics finds justification among the many studies of the student in the fact that it is the language of science. Anyone who has taken a course in chemistry, physics, or astronomy knows that these subjects are in fact math courses. Like the student who tries to read the *Odyssey* in Greek without knowing the classical Greek language, the student who tries to study physics without knowing mathematics will experience great woe with vexation of spirit. Therefore, the study of mathematics should be approached as the learning of another language. Instead of words being used for symbols, numbers and variables are used. Since the mathematical symbols can only determine either yes or no, the student should be made to recognize this limitation with mathematics and should not expect any more from the tautological discipline.

Never allow the student to use a calculator with any course in mathematics. The student must learn the processes of mathematics, which is the grammar of its unique language. In the elementary grades, the young student should become proficient with arithmetic. At this stage, the student will need to do a lot of memorizing, particularly of multiplication and division tables and the various operations. At the junior high school level, the educator should introduce a course in logic. Even though logic is associated with philosophy, logic is also called "discrete mathematics" and uses symbols for sentences and variables. The student's work with symbols, arguments, and truth tables will provide a good transition into algebra.

For the vast majority of students, the study of arithmetic and logic would suffice for a lifetime of not getting shortchanged.

13. The Curriculum: Enriching the Mind with Mathematics

Unfortunately, students who wish to go to college must take entrance exams, either for admission or for placement. Also, state school boards incorrectly assume that a student who does not have a certain amount of units in mathematics is unfit for American society and the global economy. Therefore, the student must take some mathematics in order to pass the entrance exams and the state's scrutiny. Frankly, algebra and Euclidean geometry are the only necessary courses in mathematics to ensure a tolerable score on the college entrance exams. If the state does not require a certain number of units in mathematics, then the student's career in mathematics can come to an end after two years. A few months before students take a college entrance exam, they should study—not just read, *but study*—one of the excellent ACT or SAT guides found in bookstores. These guides will show the student how to eliminate all of the wrong answers without having to solve for the correct one. Sadly, the examinations do not test for mathematical knowledge but rather determine whether the student can successfully manipulate the tests.

In the third and fourth year of the student's secondary education, the extra hour (or two) gained after being freed from mathematical oppression should be used profitably with more reading, writing, and speaking. On the other hand, if the school boards control the home school concerning the curriculum requirements, then the educator may be forced to do some creative curriculum development. As mathematical concepts are explored, the student should become acquainted with the men behind the process. For an example, the third math course of the high school student emphasizes analytical geometry. After learning the process involved, the student should read a biography about Descartes. Biographies about Pythagoras, Euclid, Cantor, Pascal, and others should be part of the readings of the student.

Along with the biographies, the educator should not neglect to have the student read the several histories of mathematics. These histories are very interesting, because from the histories, the student will become aware of the various mathematical systems used by different cultures. Egyptian, Chinese, Babylonian, and Mayan cultures had fascinating systems for counting. The student can be introduced to the several kinds of abacuses, or counting boards. Each culture had a different version. The biographies, the histories, and the multifarious systems will reveal to the student that mathematics is used primarily for "the mechanical arts," as stated by Descartes, and is properly relegated to the realm of vocational training.

But what if the student wants to be a chemist, a physicist, or an engineer? In the first place, students seldom know precisely what they will be doing ten years from now. Desires and wishes change as often as the seasons. It is the rare young person who can map out a strategy for a lifetime during the teenage years. Any job can be learned; on the other hand, the love for reading, writing, and speaking must be cultivated. Second, if they still want to participate in "the mechanical arts," then students will be able to take all the math courses they want in college. But as mentioned before, America does not need more doctors, political scientists, economists, or engineers. What America—and more precisely, the local community—needs are political and educational leaders. Pure education is not for training young people for jobs but for educating thinkers for local, state, and national governments and for colleges and universities. Any material that fails to add wisdom must be either

13. The Curriculum: Enriching the Mind with Mathematics

minimized or eliminated from students' studies and replaced with those materials that will help them to love God and neighbor.

14 THE CURRICULUM
Enriching the Senses with the Sciences

'My name is Ozymandias, King of Kings:
Look on my Works, ye Mighty, and despair!'

—PERCY BYSSHE SHELLEY, *"Ozymandias"*

O Timothy, keep that which is committed to thy trust, avoiding profane and vain babblings, and oppositions of science falsely so called.

—1 TIMOTHY 6:20

While *strength* sometimes qualifies mental or emotional resolve, the word is used most often as a quality found in the physical realm. The massive statue of Ozymandias was a reminder to all that the king was strong, as evinced by his monument and his army. However, when the modern traveler in Shelley's sonnet read the ancient inscription on the base of the now crumbling statute of the Egyptian king, the irony remains overwhelming. As empires have come and gone, as nations have come and gone, yea, even as people have come and gone, the grand, magnificent statute of Ozymandias decayed into "trunkless legs," while near the base lies the "shattered visage." The great king erected the statue as a witness to his conquering of nature by feats of engineering and by the subjugation of people. But nature has the last laugh. Why should anyone fear a trunkless and decapitated wreak? The works and the greatness of Ozymandias are gone and forgotten. However, while his physical marvels and his tyranny are no longer to be feared or dreaded, Ozymandias still offers a timely warning to everyone: human pride ends with destruction.

In these modern times, science offers its own touch of irony. While science has proven beneficial to human life, the same knowledge has proven destructive to life as well. No one complains when an arduous task is simplified or when several steps of a process are eliminated by a machine, unless unemployed workers say something. But industrialists assure the human resources that they are quite mistaken; they are not unemployed, but merely *displaced*. After they train for a better job, all will be well. Of course, research and technology provide useful conveniences in industry, in farming, and in the home. In fact, no one questions the immeasurable good that scientists have done by categorizing physical observations into clearer and more accessible bodies of knowledge. If scientists remained contented with creating new toys for consumers to play with, then Americans would have nothing to despair. However, the largest consumer is the national government with its military. The scientific research for this consumer centers on better ways to control the population, which has gotten so large that it is becoming more difficult to control. The government spends millions of dollars to research artificial intelligence as part of the programs

14. The Curriculum: Enriching the Senses with the Sciences

under the Internal Revenue Service and the armed forces. Indeed, AI is now everywhere, making the notion of "social credit scores" a reality as in China. Research in the areas of psychological, biological, and nuclear warfare is hardly worthy of a Department of Defense. By having their cabinet members head a Department of War, at least the earlier American presidents were honest enough to recognize the purpose of armies and navies.

The study of any science has but one purpose: to get a job in the world technocracy. The American technocracy is concerned about students performing well in mathematics and science, because lagging behind in technology will threaten the nation's markets for its surplus production of unnecessary goods and services. For this reason, the overemphasis of mathematics and science in the public school is the leading factor for the foundation of vocational training. Students memorize facts and processes in the social sciences, mathematical sciences, and biological, chemical, and physical sciences. The language arts have been reduced to a student's ability to read a newspaper or the operating instructions of a machine. The public schools have further entrenched the vocational purpose of education by providing instruction in daycare services with students running centers on the campus and allowing students to participate in vocational extensions, which allow them to be dismissed from classes in order to work in the community. Having students learn the process of a job is fine. But deceiving students by telling them that they are being educated is a fraud of the worst sort.

But this fraud has been called good by many able defenders, perhaps the best of the apologists being Thomas Huxley. Living his life during the nineteenth century, Huxley coined the term *agnostic*, which he applied to himself. With his zealous acceptance and popularization of evolutionary theory, Huxley was known as "Darwin's bulldog." While he derided the classical scholars as "Levites in charge of the ark of culture and monopolists of liberal education," Huxley himself was a product of a classical education, since he could quote both the Bible and classical literature as well as any preacher or scholar in his day. Yet, Huxley concedes in his speech, "Science and Culture," that the purpose of science is to provide job opportunities.

We may take it for granted then, that, in the opinion of those best qualified to judge, the diffusion of thorough scientific education is an absolutely essential condition of industrial progress; and that the College which has been opened to-day will confer an inestimable boon upon those whose livelihood is to be gained by the practice of the arts and manufactures of the district.

The occasion for this speech was the establishment of the Science College at Birmingham (England) in 1880. Huxley mentions that the founder, Sir Josiah Mason, banished three spheres of human endeavor from the school. Central to the prohibitions was that the students were not to receive an education based on literature. The next two prohibitions naturally and logically follow from the first: the students were not to engage in discussions about politics or about theology. Of course, if the sole purpose of the school is to train students in a livelihood, then reading about and discussing ideas are indeed unimportant. Yet Huxley believes that "an exclusively scientific education" leads to "attaining real culture" just as well as a literary one. But a culture cannot be maintained, much less attained, without values. Science has led not to culture, but rather to war. Incredibly, when he offers an example how science is superior to both the mind and the spirit, Huxley uses an analogy about war!

14. The Curriculum: Enriching the Senses with the Sciences

Considering progress only in the "intellectual and spiritual sphere," I find myself wholly unable to admit that either nations or individuals will really advance, if their common outfit draws nothing from the stores of physical science. I should say that an army, without weapons of precision and with no particular base of operations, might more hopefully enter upon a campaign on the Rhine, than a man, devoid of a knowledge of what physical science has done in the last century, upon a criticism of life.

Nevertheless, being a literary man himself, Huxley has to admit that a purely scientific course of study would produce lopsided men. Darwin's bulldog consoles himself that the college will offer English, French, and German, through which he thinks students will be exposed to plenty of literary culture. But since any discussion about politics or religion is prohibited, the value of the literature is denigrated to yes or no answers on tests.

On the other hand, pure education, with its emphasis on literature, culture, and values, is perceived as ill-fitting for students who must take their place in the world's economy. This is pure bunkum. If students were to study only the Bible, Latin, Greek, and ancient literature, they would be more than equipped to become any scientist or technician they desire. Science is about job training and processes, whether the process is doctoring, engineering, or administering. Any student that has the mind to read Cicero in Latin can surely learn how to construct a building or file a scrap of paper. What do students miss if they never learn Boyle's law centered on gasses and pressure? *Nothing*. Life goes merrily on its way. On the other hand, what do students miss if they fail to read *Silas Marner*? Unless they peruse from another source, the student misses *life*.

The concern that students will not be able to compete in the global marketplace is a sham for two reasons. First, students are led to believe that they will have a vital role to play in business and in public policy, when in reality, they are expendable. And second, students think that competition for markets is a wholesome exercise; yet such behavior between modern nations has created wars. The real concern of the technocrats is how will the United States ever be able to dump its excess, burdensome baggage, whether that baggage is either cheap trinkets or even cheaper human resources. Everything is an acceptable loss, except money. Small businesses, small farmers, unborn children, even soldiers are expendable to the modern nation-state. Propaganda, or advertising, is necessary to convince the citizens that the country has enemies and that a strong national defense is essential in this dangerous world.

However, the real enemies of the citizens of any nation-state are the scientists and the technocrats who make the policies while the citizens do the working and the dying. Today, technocrats base political decisions on their fear of the common citizen, who is getting tired of being a slave to the industrial-governmental cartel. The so-called strong national defense becomes ironic when the national politicians must defend their paranoia by using the Department of Defense against the nation's citizens. Men and women of ideas and biblical morality are not paranoid, and for this reason such individuals need to be placed in the most important roles of leadership.

The world has allowed Huxley plenty of time to test his belief that "for the purpose of attaining real culture, an exclusively scientific education is at least as effectual as an exclusively literary education." The result has been 140 years of the worst bloodshed since the flood. Apparently, technocrats and scientists are capable of offering leadership for dying, but not for living. The reason for

14. The Curriculum: Enriching the Senses with the Sciences

this inability for scientists to lead the living centers on the fact that science is trapped in the physical world and cannot escape from its domain. While it reigns supreme with the senses, science fails to influence the mind, the soul, or the heart. Anything that cannot be experienced by the senses must rely on another domain for its justification. For an example, researchers may observe the many effects of love, but the same researchers cannot begin to explain *what is love*, unless they drop the role of scientist and become a philosopher. To even argue that science provides the best way to know about the world is doubtful. Human senses can be very unreliable. Sight, touch, and hearing are often fooled. While walking through a graveyard at night, many a young lad will swear that he saw something, that he heard something, and that he felt something, which he believed should be better left unsolved as he ran home.

All eyewitnesses are absolutely sure that their version of the accident is correct, though all the accounts differ in details. One's common sense suggests that the earth is flat, not round. However, students are told that the world is round, even though they have *no personal* verification of the fact. Yet even though their walking or driving tell them that the surface is flat, every student dutifully writes "true" to the statement, "The earth is round." Therefore, the physical world limits answers to any question with *correct/incorrect*, or regarding processes, *on/off*, based upon the current consensus of scientists. The outdated processes of bleeding patients and of placing one's face in the numbers of a fullback to make a tackle used to have the loyal consensus of doctors and coaches. The consensus of both processes led to many unnecessary deaths and injuries.

On the other hand, the world of ideas is boundless and is not restricted by anything physical. The answers in this realm are not merely *correct* or *incorrect*. One cannot simply pull a switch to get the correct answer. Since values from the culture are paramount, ideas are either acceptable or unacceptable depending on whether the ideas represent truth or error. In order to determine truth, humans need more than a process to guide them. To suggest that the perceptions, attitudes, and desires of individual men, women, and children can be reduced to a body of scientific knowledge that provides *yes/no* answers is insanity. However, if a government is a technocracy, then life is reduced to *yes/no* answers. The citizens are told what to do, but they are not free. Theories in economics, sociology, psychology, or any other "science falsely so called" become dangerous when the scientists leave their realm of physical observation and begin declaring their findings as metaphysical truth. Anyone who claims that thousands of life-supporting planets exist in the universe without one single piece of tangible evidence is no longer a classifier of knowledge; he is simply a liar.

What allows this sanctioned chicanery is science's foundation of guessing. Whether one calls the activity a theory, a hypothesis, or a supposition, the operation is simply hazarding a guess. A scientist's conclusion on any issue is acceptable only to its greater probability and never based on its absolute proof. We accept the idea that no two snowflakes are alike, not because it is a fact, but because observed snowflakes did not duplicate one another. However, to prove the statement would be impossible, because science is incapable of performing the task of observing *every* snowflake ever produced. A legal system suffers from this lack of absoluteness. Even though the prosecutor can prove that the bullet that killed the victim came from the gun of the defendant, and that the defendant was in the vicinity at the time of the murder, and that the defendant

14. The Curriculum: Enriching the Senses with the Sciences

had a motive to kill the victim, all of this is moot if the defendant is the victim of being framed by someone else. Regarding defendants, only they and God know the truth of guilt or innocence. When the jury renders its verdict, the decision is the jury's best guess. Therefore, blind justice sometimes does make a mistake. In like manner, Columbus made his best guess about where the East Indies were and headed west. The great explorer made a miscalculation, but others benefited from Columbus's mistake and continued on from that point. This is one nice feature about science: the knowledge is convergent and is readily passed on to the next generation without a need to start from scratch. But where to go from here is anyone's guess.

Like the study of mathematics, chances are that the boards of education in most states require a certain number of units in science before students are deemed ready to take their place in American society. If this is the case, then the educator should have the student do the minimum of sciences, usually biology and chemistry. If students are concerned about getting a good job and think physics will help them, the fact is high school physics barely qualifies them to cook hamburgers. In addition to this, the study of college mathematics and sciences are not dependent upon high school courses in these subjects. Under pure education, the sciences are to be only tolerated as a whim from unenlightened technocrats. Indeed, when a self-righteous busybody begins to demand the amending of the U.S. Constitution to eliminate the electoral college, no one is going to refer to the periodic table or to a list of the names of the bones in the human body. The debate will be over whether the U.S. Constitution is a fixed contract or a living, evolving document. In other words, the debate will take place in the metaphysical world of ideas, not in the physical world of science.

Related to this discussion about science, the home school should consider having the student tend a garden. Even if the available space is enough for only one tomato plant, the student should become acquainted with how plants grow. A student's working with seeds, plants, soil, and the seasons will provide more knowledge about science than any textbook ever will. The student will learn about the major families of plants, knowing that each related plant shares the same characteristics regarding nutrients and care. The knowledge of insects, both bad and good, gives a special awareness about how insects contribute to human survival. The student will learn about caring for the soil, not by abusing it with chemical fertilizers but by supplying it with compost, the necessary ingredient for successful plants in the life and death cycle of all living things. Another benefit for students is that they will exercise their bodies. Gardening is not easy work. But to be able to sink one's hands into a soil rich in humus and to witness the first bean plants pushing their way to the surface are experiences that only the soul can appreciate. This is the stuff of poetry. But the greatest benefit of all is that the student will learn to achieve some self-reliance as well as the much-needed realization that food does not just appear on the shelves in grocery stores. If families can at least produce their own food, Americans will reclaim a large portion of their independence. The garden should be a family affair.

Also, physical exercise should not be neglected. Just taking a walk through the woods or down the street does wonders for the body. Weight lifting, swimming, and bicycling are good ways to exercise. Again, family activities are better than students exercis-

14. The Curriculum: Enriching the Senses with the Sciences

ing by themselves. Nearly 30 percent of teenagers are overweight, which undoubtedly is the result from eating unwisely and from sitting while gaming or surfing the internet. Even though Alexander Stephens and Alexander Pope are exceptions of brilliant souls who suffered poor health during their entire life, a sound body helps with mental activities. As pointed out in chapter 6, work is being performed whenever the body is physically exerting itself. Therefore, chores such as taking out the trash, cleaning the carpet, and mowing the grass are related to work and bodily exercise.

One area that is sorely neglected in science is the use of weapons. Indeed, one important mark of the gentleman was being a skilled warrior, as Castiglione states in his *Book of the Courtier*. Officers in the American military are still referred to as "officers and gentlemen." Castiglione states, "I am of opinion that the principal and true profession of the Courtier ought to be that of arms; which I would have him follow actively above all else, and be known among others as bold and strong, and loyal to whomsoever he serves." Today, "whomsoever he serves" will be the family of the gentleman. Both young men and women should be familiar with various weapons, their uses, their limitations, and particularly their safety. All gun clubs and police organizations offer lessons in the use and safety of firearms. The use of the bow and arrow should also be encouraged, as well as learning one of the martial arts. This is not to say the student should become an avid hunter, but there is something to be said about having venison and a couple of wild turkeys in the freezer. A knowledge of weapons and self-defense is like a fire hydrant; one hopes that it will never be used, but it is nice to know that the hydrant is there just in case the house catches fire. The times are perilous to be sure, and self-defense of one's family is always prudent. Like gardening and exercising, self-defense should be a joint project of the family.

This critique has admittedly been critical of technology and science. The criticism would not be justified if technocrats and scientists were contented simply to shuffle paper. However, the paper-shufflers are convinced that they know what is best for the rest of us. These rogues are the ultimate busybodies, interfering in the lives of millions of parents, who know exactly what is best for their own families.

The greatest arrogance shown by any person is the contemptible belief that human technology and science can solve all moral and intellectual bankruptcy. Unfortunately, with no ideas to live for or to think with, technocrats fine-tune the economies of the world into warfare where, much to their relief, right and wrong are suspended for the human race for a spell. In George Bernard Shaw's *Arms and the Man*, Sergius understood this insanity when he states, "I won the battle the wrong way when our worthy Russian generals were losing it the right way. That upset their plans and wounded their self-esteem." Actually, the modern industrial state does not really care if it wins or loses, because the flow of money continues regardless of the outcome. On the other hand, when things do not go as planned, the technocrat with a wounded self-esteem is dangerous to all free people. Beware! Science will be called forth to rescue peaceful citizens from their worst enemies—themselves. But nature has a way of humbling tyrants eventually; therefore, oppressors should carefully consider Ozymandias's warning, "Look on my Works, ye Mighty, and despair!"

Wars are inevitable. But this does not mean that gangs of politicians should be licensed to go out of their way to pick a fight.

14. The Curriculum: Enriching the Senses with the Sciences

Pure education produces young men and women who can govern themselves well, and such men and women can provide the necessary leadership in the government, schools, and homes. More technology, more trinkets, and more science will not solve the terrible bloodshed of peaceful citizens. Men and women with reliable ideas of morality, a firm resolve to enrich their culture, and gentle conduct toward others can at least restore some sanity in confused and reckless government in homes, churches, universities, and politics.

FINAL THOUGHTS

And there she lulled me asleep
And there I dream'd—Ah! woe betide!—
The latest dream I ever dreamt
On the cold hill side.

—JOHN KEATS, *"La Belle Dame sans Merci"*

Wherefore, beloved, seeing that ye look for such things, be diligent that ye may be found of him in peace, without spot, and blameless.

—2 PETER 3:14

Nothing is more frustrating than agreeing with the ideas of a philosopher or a teacher but then discovering the ideas to be impracticable, when theory cannot be translated into practical life and daily living. It would be better to have a millstone tied around our necks and thrown into the sea than to live with great ideas that cannot be implemented. Such disappointment leads to a greater bitterness toward life. Indeed, this vexation results in dreams of utopian madness. But pure education is not like the woman who lulls the knight to sleep in Keats's poem. Nor is pure education the dream that the knight witnessed with kings, princes, and warriors having "starved lips." The realm of pure education is happily for the living, not for the dead.

The ideas in this book show that the purely educated student ought to become the best of all possible citizens. The educator is key, who must be an example to her students. In order to teach patience and self-control, the educator must likewise show these qualities in her dealings with her students and others. Her students will be young ladies and gentlemen who will have genuine manners, a love for true beauty, and an appreciation for the brevity of life. Time will not be wasted, but rather it will be employed in contemplation, reading, composing, and exercise. A sound mind, a kind demeanor, and a good name will be preferred over a lust for money. Not being enslaved to the tyranny of enforced vocational and social training, students will have a greater flexibility in order to develop their heart, soul, mind, and senses. In addition to this, the student can take advantage of the superior Hebrew tradition as well as the Western tradition when this tradition supports and clarifies. Best of all, the world will make sense, and the student can become actively involved, enriching neighbors, community, and culture. Because of their privileged status of being educated, purely educated students will be the natural leaders in government, colleges, and homes.

But now just suppose for the sake of argument that all public and private schools disappear and that all education is now conducted in the homes. With all of these leaders being educated, eventually every position in government and the universities will be filled. Then what? This situation assumes that all home schools will use pure education. In order for this to happen, every house-

Final Thoughts

hold would have to adopt the Hebrew tradition for its school as primary, and the Western tradition as an adjunct. But suppose this is the case. Who will become the laborers in the society? Not everyone can be leaders in such a situation. True, but there will be true leadership and examples in nearly all of the homes again. When such a situation occurs, the mega-corporations will disappear, since the citizens would be educated not to buy unnecessary stuff. The entertainment industry along with most sporting events will disappear. Large cities will become rare. Companies will be smaller and will be decentralized, producing enough goods for their particular region. The agrarian life will become a viable alternative to millions of people again, who will desire a greater independence and the simplicity of rural life, which offers stability, purpose of life, and a solid legacy for one's progeny. Individuals will become self-sufficient, and for them to accept a dole would be an insult to their dignity. All phases of life will be governed by individuals who know how to govern themselves well. Universities will get back to teaching human beings to be human, and colleges will be out of the vocational-training business. Those who desire to work for others will find owners of factories and land to be fair and just individuals. The government of purely educated men will allow the maximum freedom and will interfere in the affairs of others only when absolutely necessary. There will be no criminal class, because the judgment of crime will be swift and certain. Children will play without fear, possessions will be respected, and citizens will enjoy a freedom never experienced in humankind's history except when Adam and Eve were in the Garden of Eden.

What I have just described is the way life will be on the earth during the future reign of the Lord Jesus Christ. However, until that time, it is very doubtful that Americans will ever achieve such a glorious life as suggested above apart from divine intervention. Today, what the home educator must focus on is not the society at large, but rather each individual student under her charge. Indeed, this is the only domain with which she should primarily be concerned. This narrow scope of responsibility will permit the educator to ensure that her students are at peace with God and will be prepared to meet Him blameless and spotless.

Timendi causa est nescire.
Ignorance is the cause of fear.

APPENDIX
The Educator and Cultural Reclamation

by James Everett Kibler, Ph.D.

Upon reading this work, I am struck by its similarities to the sound philosophy of the landmark *I'll Take My Stand* (1930), whose authors valued tradition, and defined the good life as a whole life, not a life of mere leisure. They and Watson would most certainly agree with the poet John Keats that life is a journey in the "vale of soul-making," the process of attempting to grow a soul to health, beauty, perfection, and wholeness. It should be remembered, after all, that the words *health*, *whole*, and *holy* stem from the same root. Watson tells us in his chapter on "Enriching the Soul with Literature," that "Americans have redefined leisure to exclude intellectual activity, and therefore they have truly buried themselves alive." He continues perceptively: "The central discipline that makes education different from technical training is missing in the schools." Neither soul, heart, nor emotions are nourished there. And, indeed, if they are not, the person is not a student but a mere automaton, a mechanized user of machines. I am here reminded of a very fine essay by the poet James Dickey, entitled "Computerized Rape in the Vale of Soul-Making" on precisely the same subject.

As Watson shows, our colleges and universities (both major or minor) have drifted toward becoming glorified tech schools, for the training up of technicians for Big Business and Big Industry. These trainee-apprentices are educated at taxpayers' expense, quite a sweet deal for Big Business and Big Industry, which arguably should be doing this at their own expense, instead of subverting colleges from their proper and legitimate goals. Money aside, it is far more serious to see what this tech-style training does to the college and university. Indeed, the soul, heart, and emotions are oftentimes missing in the equation.

Another crucial problem pointed out here is that too often from high school to college "the goal of the student is to get a good job." I might add that this automatically involves a knee-jerk "going where the job is," rather than going back home to strengthen one's own native community. Our greatest living American author, Wendell Berry, has written that what our colleges should be giving today is a "homecoming degree," in other words, fitting the student to go home, rather than where the job and highest pay are.

All our government-supported schools, both high and low, are on balance supremely anti-traditional. They more often than not undermine and attack all traditional values to the extent of even deconstructing the idea that there can be any such term except as a means of oppression. So bizarre and extreme the world of education has become today! As Watson shows, what now passes for education is usually a sorry and hollow technical substitute perpetrated by technocrats in a technocratic empire.

Appendix: The Educator and Cultural Reclamation

A real education, as John Gould Fletcher wrote in his excellent chapter on the subject in *I'll Take My Stand*, should help the student to become a citizen of the world with his spiritual roots grounded in the local—that is, home—in the community where he was born and raised. Realistically, this message cannot be expected to issue from professors who, after all, have made many moves, have "gone where the job is," and whose only real home is now career or the chosen specialties they research and teach. In that fact lies the magnitude of the problem.

The anti-traditional underminers of humanity have had their way unchecked in our time to the extent that when most students reach college, they have moved many times and have little or no concept of home or community. Their parents have merely followed the modern mantra and "gone where the job is." They have made their work their home. And what confusion results! Many university students today are quite angry over this situation. Their complaint with fathers and mothers who have "gone where the job is" six or seven times in their eighteen years is more than youthful rebellion. Their disgruntlement is valid, and, I might add, reason for hope that times may change. But it will also take pressure on Big Business and Big Industry to alter their policies toward employees to include the right to the stability of place and community, in other words, not to be made to move on demand, or be punished for not doing so.

The failure of modern education, high and low, rises out of this core of anti-traditionalism, reflecting unfortunately the essential anti-traditionalism of the times—sold to us in the false packaging of "progress." In this vacuum, what wonder Virgil is not read, Virgil whose very center is love and valuing of home. What wonder the

Classics go untaught and unread. The typical modern would have trouble even understanding the concept of the *genius loci*, the spirit of place. Southern writers understand and depict it well, however; and yes, indeed, literature from Virgil to Wendell Berry can help the disembodied, deracinated student at least to get a notion of what home can mean, and the values of a real many-generational involvement with a place and its traditions.

William G. Simms, the father of Southern literature, said it best in 1842: "a nomadic society is by necessity a barbarous one." To him, the first requirement for the creation of high civilization was "staying put." The barbarism of our own modern times is arguably a result of a failure to see Simms's truth, and our embracing this sort of drifting, this essential rootlessness.

The one word that comes to mind when I think of our time is *deracination*. How very telling it is that the word is so applicable as summation of the era that it is never even used. Indeed, real deracination is so common, so pervasive, that we all take it for granted, like oxygen, as if it were some unquestionable great good, as if there were no alternative way. Most moderns do not even know the meaning of the term.

Establishment educators are the most nomadic of creatures, particularly educators of the university kind. Give many of them a few dollars more or some greater prestige, and they are gone. For some, I wonder if they fully unpack. When one's home becomes one's job, when one's home is one's career or one's art, this of course makes good sense. In this rootless, nomadic, supremely anti-traditional time, one's duty is to what enhances oneself— and with little real regard to the places, the communities, through which one passes, like some accidental tourist.

Appendix: The Educator and Cultural Reclamation

Is it enough that one feels he is doing "missionary work" in bringing the light to those laboring in the dark? Truly, the arrogance of the anti-traditional progressive is as great as Everest, is as great as his ignorance of or disregard for place. For those do not truly bring light who prevent seeing the value of the place where we put down our feet.

And it need not necessarily be this way with educators. The old Celtic bards of highest caste, the Old Irish *filidh* by name, were transient but trained in law, religion, legends, music, genealogy, history, and verse. They made poems and stories of all local things for the patrons they stayed among. Their knowledge of geography was particularly intimate, and their store of *faoín dúlraidh* (songs in praise of place) was large and especially highly regarded. Many of these songs were associated with holy places—certain trees, rocks, hills (like Tara), rivers, etc. and so that there arises in teacher and listener alike, a close love of the locale and a sense of its holiness. The Irish even have a name for this love, *duchás*, defined by James Flannery as "the intimate attachment fostered through stories associated with a particular place." For the Irish, this deep love of one's native place has been passed down through centuries; and it all was owing largely to bardic "professors," who invested place with histories, legends, and meanings that created a spiritual aura of reverence for the dwellers therein. They forged a sacred bond between the people and the land and an understanding that the world is holy.

These bardic teachers were the very keepers of tradition and provided the stability and continuity that civilized. And they were properly, rightly, the most respected of men. Master poets bore the name *ollamh*, still the word for "professor" in the Irish language.

As James Flannery points out, there was tremendous difference between the "overtly programmatic education of today" and the "fierce intellectual and spiritual discipline" of the ancient apprentice scholar-artists of that day. The students lived in sparsely furnished tiny huts. The single candle was reserved only for special occasions. Contemplation was central, so as to engage the soul as well as the mind, and to mate spiritual and aesthetic enlightenment. The ancients, now more than ever, thus have much to teach us in our fragmented, empiricist, over-specialized day.

Watson is very good at sketching out what makes an educated person and how that person must strive for wholeness. His values are soundly traditional in an unsettled time. Homeschooling is an obvious combatant of the homeless, deracinated age, at a time when most Americans are essentially "the homeless"; while government schools, as Watson shows, generally inculcate a mindset that strengthens the abstract allegiance to a leviathan State at the expense of other things. The ever-present carrot is a presumed economic payoff for the exchange of the integrated whole. This is a most American "Yankee" thing, in the stereotypical extreme!

Brought up in such an environment, what wonder the increasing instability and dissatisfaction of the young; what wonder the confusion and fragmented sensibility of the times. The integrated sensibility must be nurtured and grown in this vale of soul-making. It starts in the home, an anchored known place. It grows with the guidance of parents and grandparents, neighbors and kin, and the more-or-less wise. Its object is not material advancement and the things of this world, placed above all. It does not "go where the job is" without first considering deeply the trade-off of what will be lost.

Appendix: The Educator and Cultural Reclamation

Andrew Lytle, another wise author in *I'll Take My Stand*, said that one can tell a Southerner by the question he usually asks when greeting a stranger. "Where are you from?" he asks; while the non-Southerner usually inquires, "What do you do?" This is a great cultural divide. But the most Southern of Southerners, Lytle added, would ask, "Where do your people bury?" In this last, we see the center of tradition and home understanding, and the opposite of modern deracination. If education is to be revived, and the culture too, it will most likely come on Southern soil, or at least from this Southern sensibility—the essence of traditionalism.

Wendell Berry has written that throughout our history, the great American divide has been over the question of whether to go or to stay. A real educator will explore this fact, have his students weigh the consequences of the choice, and not automatically assume the former.

Modern education, high and low, has perhaps been the supreme failure of our times in not questioning the material values pervasive in society, and dismally failing to encourage the young to appreciate the value of what is at the doorstep, the local—the homely local, if you will. Far from giving homecoming degrees, it has too often done everything in its power to undermine the same. It is high time for a change.

Truly, as Watson declares, literature can provide us one key. I would recommend the essays of Berry for a start, perhaps his *Sex, Economy, Freedom, and Community*; *Another Turn of the Crank*; *Home Economics*; *The Unsettling of America*; *The Gift of Good Land*; *A Continuous Harmony*; *Standing by Words*; or *What Are People For?* I have successfully taught all these titles to college students, but any of his collections would serve. Then his novels *The Memory of Old*

Jack and his most recent *Jayber Crow* will dramatize such a stable life rooted on the soil and the sacred bond to place it engenders, to those who otherwise might not have a clue as to what this is. Who knows? Staying put might just be so novel and foreign a concept that it might become trendy—a good trend for a change. After all, as traditionalists know, there is nothing new under the sun.

If students were to develop stay-at-home "home desires," their craving for things could be moderated, in order to live "economically" on a planet with limited and ever-shrinking resources. The squandering practiced and encouraged by our throw-away, planned-obsolescent society has also come down to throwing away place. The modern credo is too often "Discard this home for a new one." "Discard this place for another." "Move on; move up." "Throw the old away in the name of progress." This is the throw-away society in just one more destructive phase. Such a process is not recycling, but results in a dead-end culture of death that is no culture at all, and leads nowhere but to emptiness and distraction and the vapid and sordid bread and circuses (Juvenal's *panem et circenses* during that other empire) of sports, pop culture, sexual titillation, and scandal keeping the masses pacified and diverted from the important issues. Watson's comments on the necessity to teach self-discipline and self-control are very apt in this context.

At the core of the new education should be a redefining of the term *success*. The current assumption is too often materially based. If the dad or mom ever on the move has reached a suburban house with six telephones, four bathrooms, and a fully stocked three-car garage, success is assumed. Built by and for transients, the best and most exclusive gated real estate development is still not a community after all. When success is defined in this exclusively material way, there is dangerous rot at the core. This is particularly the case when the children do not know their grandparents or cousins, or only see them but one time a year, when the children have no long-term friends, no sense of a family home-place or multi-generational family tradition, and question quite honestly who they are. The culturally deprived are now the real poverty class in a land where the stomach is usually filled. Genuine poverty centers should spring up nationwide to administer to these pitiful poor, and to address such a problem, so dire and extreme.

A very wise Southern author gave this definition of success fifty years ago in a very great memoir: "Success is the *how*, not *how much* of achievement." It is *being* rather than *having*. This understanding involves the moral, the spiritual, whole person—one might say, the *properly educated* person. I wonder how many business schools in our colleges have thought to deal honestly, or are capable of dealing honestly, with that definition. And so here we return to Watson's thesis. Real education must be more than a technical training. Watson, to his credit, makes room for the moral, spiritual man, and puts the lie to the extreme relativism of a surface and superficial secular humanism which has too often become the educator's own pseudo-religion.

Education of Watson's design builds the basis for a homecoming degree, where the one seeking home, and coming home, is made fit to inhabit home. No higher praise could be given to an educator in this evil, anti-traditional time, when science-based materialism has created a virtual machine-culture, a fragmented, hedonistic, deracinated, technocratic, egocentric era that in its arrogance thinks it is the zenith of accomplishment, and where the shell of life is hollow of its kernel and meat.

Watson's modest volume faces hard facts and gives proper warnings. His is a prophetic book that takes its authority from a broad vision of wholeness and the elegant simplicity of good common sense. It is one of those books that has the potential to do immense good.